Boost Your
Presentation IQ

Praise for Boost Your Presentation IQ

"Whether you are you giving a presentation in front of 500 people or for 3 people in a meeting, your personal presentation style and speaking abilities will enhance or detract from the point your are trying to make. Marilyn Pincus shows you how to have impact whether you are speaking for 5 minutes or 6 hours!"

—Joan Burge
Founder and CEO
Office Dynamics, Ltd.

"Help on every page for even the most poised and experienced presenter/communicator. This book's arrangement and format signal a fresh approach to a subject that bedevils us all in this age of so much information and so little meaning and relevancy—how to effectively reach our audiences. Read it, learn and communicate."

—Paul M. Sanchez, ABC, APR
Communication Business Leader
Mercer Human Resource Consulting
Europe

"Meeting planners pay fees of $50,000 and more for celebrity speakers. Fame alone won't make the sale. These speakers perfected their presentation skills. Marilyn Pincus unveils strategies every great speaker uses."

—Angela Schelp
Executive Speakers Bureau

Boost Your Presentation IQ

Marilyn Pincus

McGraw-Hill

New York   Chicago   San Francisco
Lisbon   London   Madrid   Mexico City
Milan   New Delhi   San Juan   Seoul
Singapore   Sydney   Toronto

1 2 3 4 5 6 7 8 9 0   FGR/FGR   0 9 8 7 6 5

ISBN 0-07-145898-0

McGraw-Hill books are available at special discounts to use as premiums and sales promotions, or for use in corporate training programs. For more information, please write to the Director of Special Sales, Professional Publishing, McGraw-Hill, Two Penn Plaza, New York, NY 10121-2298. Or contact your local bookstore.

This book is printed on recycled, acid-free paper containing a minimum of 50% recycled de-inked paper.

Contents

This book is dedicated to my cherished grandchildren
Emily Beth Rosenweig
and
Vasya David Pincus

Acknowledgments

Here's to the supporting cast! An author writes the book alone, but that's where the solitude ends. Shine the spotlight on the many talented people at McGraw-Hill who put the author's rendering through dress rehearsal and ready it for opening night. Top billing in that department belongs to the editor, Ms. Donya Dickerson. Hats off to the cadre of people who work to make the book a long running hit. Finally, a round of applause is reserved for Ms. Grace E. Freedson, Literary Agent. I couldn't have done it without you. Many thanks to you all.

Introduction

In the workplace your success depends heavily upon how you're received. *How you're received dictates how recipients respond.* Based on how you present an idea, people may or may not buy something from you, may or may not learn something from you, and may or may not be disposed to conduct business with you or keep you employed!

Because you want to be well received, it's important that your presentation skills are top-notch. Discover how best to use winning presentation skills, and you'll be in a powerful position to obtain the results you desire.

Boost Your Presentation IQ takes you on a unique Q&A journey. When you reach the final destination, at the end of the book, you will have an arsenal of valuable communication techniques at your disposal.

Decisions, Decisions

Here's how this book works: Fifty questions are posed. Each one is partnered with three different scenarios—or three possible answers. You select the best answers and keep score. Brief explanations reveal why one answer is stronger than the others. Each answer receives a point assignment, and these points enable you to quickly judge your Presentation IQ. As a result, you zero in on what you need to do, how you need to do it, and why it's recommended.

Get ready to make more sales, train others to be more productive, win support from customers, clients, colleagues, and vendors, and cement your position as a valued employee. Every time you step up to make a presentation—whether in front of hundreds of people or just a few—you'll dazzle them with your ability to communicate. Not only will you get your way more often, but more people will see you as someone who inspires confidence.

Here's an illustration:

Jill Smith has been told by her boss that her staff of 10 will be moved to a new building located in a nearby town. Jill's staff is highly trained, and company executives are counting on her to motivate all these employees to make the transition to the new address. Jill knows that two of the 10 are outspoken and tend to influence the others. She considers three approaches to presenting her staff with the news.

Which is the best approach for delivering this news?

(A) Gather everyone together and announce the move to the new building. Explain why the move is necessary and how each of them will benefit by working at this new location.

(B) Prior to calling a formal meeting, talk with the two outspoken employees. Take special note of their responses. If objections surface, get permission from management to take steps to satisfy complaints that are likely to arise at the meeting.

(C) Select a different venue for this meeting. Jill Smith usually holds staff meetings in a conference room, but now she plans to invite the staff to a lunch meeting at a local restaurant. She reserves a table in a private room and arranges for the hostess to escort each employee to the table.

Approach:

(A) Adequate. This approach isn't especially creative, but it will suffice. The important point is stressing benefits.

(B) Weak. A good manager can solicit input from most or all staff members casually and without fanfare. If only one or two people are approached, it sets up an aura of intrigue and a suggestion that something bad is about to happen. Tongues start wagging and nothing positive is gained.

(C) Favored: It's important that staff members focus on the message. By inviting staff to a new meeting place, the manager underscores the importance of the message. Moreover, the restaurant site helps set the mood. "Something good is about to be announced."

Jill's actions put the spotlight on three Presentation Skills:

1. *Know your audience.* Know their objectives, their capacity to understand your message.

2. *Get their attention*: Every minute is precious, and people have short attention spans. The special meeting place acts as an unspoken attention grabber.

3. *Prepare*: Jill Smith was thinking ahead. She prepared to counter objections. Of course, one assumes that prior to the meeting she obtained permission from her boss to satisfy anticipated objections.

Rate yourself: Which one do you favor?

If you chose answer (A), give yourself 2 points.

If you chose answer (B), give yourself zero points.

If you chose answer (C), give yourself 5 points.

Add them up. How many points did you earn?

As you move through *Boost Your Presentation IQ*, tally all the points you've earned to get an indication of how you're doing. This is not a scientific method for assessing Presentation Skills, but it does provide you with a measurement tool. Are your Presentation Skills good? Could they be better? If they're already tops, good for you! You've just received a pleasant confirmation of this fact.

As you read through the explanations, you'll also notice that the definitions of Presentation Skills aren't static. *Know your audience*, for example, may be explained as paying attention to whether the audience is composed of people from a predominately different culture than your own or composed of retirees as opposed to working people. These are not the same as the *Know your audience* definitions provided in the Jill Smith illustration, which involved predicting each person's response to change. Before you know it, you'll (painlessly) acquire a broad base of information about what to consider when you want to know your audience.

At the back of the book you'll find a complete list of Presentation Skills. Refer to it when you're getting ready to make a presentation. You'll be reminded about priority points in a to-the-point style. For example, *tell them what you're going to tell them. Tell them. Tell them what you told them.* You'll find this reminder under "Prepare." This and other "At-a-Glance Reminders" are within easy reach whenever you seek a refresher.

While *Boost Your Presentation IQ* spotlights dozens of everyday type presentations such as the above example, it also offers lots of information on making presentations to large audiences. You'll find scenarios that discuss being a Keynote Speaker, Master or Mistress of Ceremonies, and so on. And you'll find ample information to boost your presentation IQ when you address audiences that number in the hundreds and thousands. Scenarios that target on-camera presentations (e.g., television appearances) and radio presentations, as well as in a theater or a large auditorium, are explored too.

Part Two of the book, "Proven Techniques for Boosting Your Presentation IQ," contains techniques, tips, and strategies that you can use to further improve your presentation skills. This section is heavy with details.

By the time you close this book, you will have been transported to every imaginable presentation venue and be equipped to exceed expectations. And then you can go ahead and take a bow. You will have earned it!

Boost Your
Presentation IQ

PART 1

The Presentation IQ Test

Popular Types of Presentations

Report, Inform, Explain, Announce

Whatever the venue—small or large—when you have information to deliver, the key point is to focus on the facts. You muddy the waters when you frequently digress to offer your opinions, make attempts to be humorous, or otherwise stray from the specifics. On those occasions when opinions are pertinent, you're well advised to save them for the end.

During these types of presentations, there are typically a lot of facts. Facts can be dry:

> The plant opens at 6:00 A.M. The new bus route includes a stop at our warehouse. Sales were off by 20 percent last quarter. Headquarters will be closed for two weeks in December and employees will receive one week's pay. Anyone eligible for vacation pay can declare the second week a vacation week and collect two weeks' pay.

When you have numerous facts to report or when complex numbers are involved, arrange for listeners to "see" them as well as hear them. A handout of some type is practical and easy to produce. Keep it simple. Make it brief. If consequences are directly related to the information you're presenting, say so. These consequences are facts too. The availability of vacation pay, in the situation mentioned above, is a perfect example. If possible, ask for questions and provide answers at the end of your presentation. If not, end by referring listeners to another forum. For example:

> This information is posted on the company Web site. You'll hear more about this from the human resources director at our regular staff meeting.

The more disciplined you are about sticking to the facts, the more successful you'll be at providing complete information. People are free to absorb the new information without distraction, and you will accomplish your mission.

Since it is likely you'll be involved in reporting, informing, explaining, or announcing on a fairly regular basis, use the first three scenarios and related questions included in this part of the Presentation IQ Test to hone your skills in these areas.

Persuade, Win Over, Sell

The next most popular type of presentation is trying to persuade your audience. Your mission here is to stimulate or inspire listeners to act. You want those individuals to believe something they didn't believe before you confronted them. A shy and retiring manner of speaking won't do the job. You'll probably present an upbeat, animated persona to listeners. You'll work to raise the energy level in the room. You'll put people in the mood to say yes. In the process, you'll do everything within your power to accentuate the positive. If objections are raised, you'll address them quickly and move on. You'll strive to endear yourself to listeners because people do business with people they like. And when you're in front of a group trying to make a sale, you're conducting business!

Entertain, Divert, Relax, Set a Mood

The final set of questions in Part 1 of the Presentation IQ Test is about the mood you want to set. Some entertainers use "warm-up" acts to set a tone, to "tweak" the atmosphere, before they arrive on stage. And there are times when you'll address a group to get them ready for the main speaker or what is coming next. Other times, however, you'll be the only speaker, and you may be responsible for everything.

Question 1

Management hired a new chef for the company cafeteria and made other improvements in order to entice more employees to stay on the premises to eat lunch. They did this in an effort to prevent lunch hours from becoming lunch hours plus 15 minutes. In spite of their efforts, many employees still left the building for lunch. The company president decided to have casual meetings with employees to call attention to the new and improved cafeteria. Should the president:

(A) Focus on the chef's qualifications. Don't omit anything that would showcase the chef's culinary talents.

(B) Present the facts in a casual way. A one-page handout can list the chef's achievements and detail one week of menu selections.

(C) Bring the chef along and introduce him or her to everyone. Arrange for the chef to be available to answer employees' questions if they seek out the chef in the cafeteria. Announce that this opportunity is available when the president makes introductions. Don't linger with any one group.

Answers

The strongest answer:

(C) This is a hospitable action that should please the chef and employees. The president's involvement with the introduction immediately establishes the chef's importance. Who could resist going to see if the chef is as good as the "boss" claims?

The adequate answer:

(A) This may be the only kind of information people need to pique their curiosity and try having lunch in the cafeteria.

The weakest answer:

(B) No one expects the company president to act like "one of the gang," and if he or she comes with nothing more than a one-page handout that touts the chef's achievements, it may appear odd. (That kind of data can be distributed in a myriad of ways: the company newsletter, paycheck stuffers, or via an e-mail announcement.) Employees would probably be suspicious of this ploy and focus on the messenger's motives instead of the message.

Rate yourself: Which one do you favor:

If you chose answer (A), give yourself 3 points.

If you chose answer (B), give yourself ½ point.

If you chose answer (C), give yourself 5 points.

Points earned: _____

The president's actions put the spotlight on three Presentation Skills:
1. **Select main points.** Deliver the most important facts.
2. **Prove it.** Be ready with evidence to support your facts.
3. **Exhibit business etiquette.** Know the protocol for making introductions.

Question 2

Sandra and Tim are senior managers employed by a company that operates grocery stores. Each has been trained to use a new computer system and is expected to teach office workers at various stores how to do the same. It's a six-month special assignment. When classes begin, they waste no time. Worksheets are distributed and Sandra makes her presentation. It's loaded with content. After a 10-minute break, Tim takes over and delivers another set of instructions. This is how they learned the new system, but they soon discover employees aren't *getting it*. Sandra says, "It will take us a year to teach everyone these skills. I'm asked so many irrelevant questions. Is it them or is it us?"

Which of the following is the best approach for instructing?

   (A) Deliver small amounts of information and follow up by asking open-ended questions. Employees learn from dialogue too.

   (B) Keep your antenna up for different values and points of view, and don't be afraid to change the way you deliver information. If employees think that new systems are a waste of time, instead of plunging ahead to instruct on their use, take time to explain why they are superior to the status quo. Then instruct.

   (C) Solve problems. Deliver the instructions or facts so students realize a tangible benefit: "Follow these instructions and shave 20 minutes off the end-of-the-day tabulations. That will get you on the highway headed home before the busiest traffic times."

Answers

The strongest answer:

(B) A good speaker takes the time to assess the audience beforehand. This assessment is typically based on experiences the speaker has had; in this case, with these employees. It's important to realize that preconceived notions can offer a false sense of security. The speaker who stays alert to body language (restlessness, grimaces) and other signs (questions, comments) indicating that listeners aren't receptive can act to remedy the situation. Should employees tour a different store to see how the new system works? It takes a confident presenter to scrap his or her method for imparting information and think "outside the box."

The adequate answer:

(A) Questions that can't be answered with a simple yes or no alert a presenter to how listeners are receiving the information. This *barometer* offers the presenter an opportunity to assess needs.

The weakest answer:

(C) At first glance this suggestion seems reasonable. But in fact this is a weak approach because it's not believable. Employees can't leave the office early because they shave 20 minutes off the end-of-the-day tabulation time.

Rate yourself: Which one do you favor?

If you chose answer **(A)**, give yourself 4 points.

If you chose answer **(B)**, give yourself 5 points.

If you chose answer **(C)**, give yourself 1 point.

Points earned: _____

Sandra and Tim's assignment put the spotlight on two Presentation Skills:
1. Control the audience.
2. Exaggeration must be handled with care.

Question 3

Several hundred people will be in the audience when Jan Herbert, a motivational speaker, takes the stage next Monday night. Jan is accustomed to speaking to groups of 30 or 40 attendees. She typically walks around the room, but this time she'll have to remain on stage. She'll need visual aids that can be seen at the back of the large auditorium, and she ponders how many things must be changed to accommodate this large group. She begins to feel as though she's a beginner instead of a seasoned professional speaker.

Which of the following is the best approach for speaking effectively to this large group?

- **(A)** Jan uses a tape recorder to practice her speech. She knows her topic well and doesn't consider what she says but rather how she says it. She jots notes on a paper: *Slow down, finish saying a word before saying the next word. Smile. I don't hear a smile when I listen.* Jan starts over and incorporates changes. When she's satisfied, she asks her partner, Barry, to listen to her speech.

- **(B)** Jan scrutinizes her visual aids. She makes inquiries and learns that her presentation can be televised and she can appear on a large screen. The audience will be able to see anything she holds in her hands, and the posters she uses will be magnified and easy to see.

- **(C)** "What shall I wear?" she frets. She is always careful about wardrobe selections and grooming when she makes appearances, but will this new venue force her to make different selections? How about makeup? Should it be applied more liberally?

Answers

The strongest answer:

(A) Voice, pace, pitch, and everything related to vocal delivery deserve a high priority. Just as ballet dancers strive to achieve perfection while knowing perfection is not possible, good speakers realize their performances are a work in progress. Jan wisely employed the "two heads are better than one" principle when she asked her partner Barry to get involved.

The adequate answer:

(B) This may be an easy way to handle the challenge, but it's still important to test the premise. What if the usual visual aids can't be seen well on the television screen? You won't know until you try.

The weakest answer:

(C) Personal appearance is important, but since Jan is a professional speaker and accustomed to preparing to look good in front of an audience. There's no reason to believe this time will be different. Of the three featured basics, this one is in last place.

Rate yourself: Which one do you favor?

If you chose answer (A), give yourself 5 points.

If you chose answer (B), give yourself 4 points.

If you chose answer (C), give yourself 1 point.

Points earned: _____

Jan's preparation helps highlight two Presentation Skills:
1. **Build your confidence.** Banish self-doubt before you step up to the microphone. You owe it to your listeners to be the best you can be. A review of basic principles comes to the rescue!
2. **Use time wisely.** Why show visual aids to people who can't see them or can't see them clearly? It's a waste of time.

Question 4

The ZYX Glass Company will merge with another company in April. The managing partner realizes it's important to quell job loss fears and speaks to the staff about it.

"I'm going to tell you something you'll probably find difficult to believe," she begins, and goes on to state what everyone in the room knows and fears: that in a typical merger, some jobs are lost. Then she adds, "Since you're the best that ZYX has to offer in this merger, your job security is not only assured, it's essential." She explains that the company's 112 employees are considered the best in the world when it comes to operating highly sophisticated glass production machinery and that their productivity record in the industry is second to none. "I can't promise you anything until papers are signed, but there's a good chance that instead of severance pay, you'll receive bonus dollars!" She smiles and shakes hands with everyone in a celebratory manner, then passes everyone a details package that contains information about the other company and lists executives' phone numbers employees can use if they have questions.

What is the best approach for persuading people that change will be good for them?

(A) Since change represents the unknown, it's often surrounded by gloom and doom forecasts and dire predictions. Give voice to these concerns. Your candor undermines worrisome whispers and damaging conjecture. Employees are less edgy and free to be productive while they wait for the pieces to fall into place.

(B) Tell people they're appreciated. Give them facts and figures to back up statements you make so your comments are accepted as genuine. This kind of communication encourages employees. Few are likely to start job hunting, which under the circumstances might be the prudent thing to do.

(C) "If it walks like a duck and quacks like a duck, it must be a duck" is a widely accepted line of reasoning. When a convincing case is made (i.e., this merger is a good thing), employees embrace the logic and believe in a promising future.

Answers

The strongest answer:
Both **(A)** and **(B)** are strong.

   (A) This approach heads off nasty gossip, which can be a powerful morale breaker. Since change is usually accompanied by a steady flow of information highs and lows, it's wise to designate well-informed and respected "go-to" people to answer questions.

   (B) Who can argue with offering praise and then backing it up with facts and figures? If you selected **(B)** as the best way to persuade employees that all is well, so be it!

The weakest answer:

   (C) There's at least one thing wrong with this approach. It doesn't go far enough. People may understand they represent the "gold standard" in the industry, but does that mean all of them are needed after the merger? Answer that question before anyone asks it.

Rate yourself: Which one do you favor?

If you chose answer **(A)**, give yourself 5 points.

If you chose answer **(B)**, give yourself 5 points.

If you chose answer **(C)**, give yourself 3 points.

Points earned: _____

The managing partner relies heavily on the following Presentation Skills:
1. **Encourage people to believe.** "You gotta believe" is a phrase closely associated with Philadelphia's late, great baseball star Tug McGraw. To persuade people to be fearless, appeal to their faith.
2. **Steal the thunder.** When you confess to a mistake you get the bad news out in the open.

Question 5

Advertising department personnel want town residents to appear in a breakfast cereal commercial. Signed consent forms must be obtained, and people are reluctant to sign them. "We can hire actors," one executive observes. Another recommends winning over residents at a town meeting: "Let's tell them we can hire actors but we'd rather showcase the town." The director of advertising gets permission to speak at the next town meeting. He knows people are proud of their quiet way of life. After he speaks, people line up to sign consent forms.

What did he say to win them over?

(A) Money *talks*. Did he donate money to the community center new roof fund?

(B) Townspeople take pride in their homes. Did the director promise to include several neighborhoods in his commercial?

(C) Maybe he appealed to their sense of history: "The commercial will capture your town as it is today. And it will be done by highly skilled professionals. Copies will be given to your library and the local historical society. And if our company uses the film years from now, the town will be entitled to royalty payments for use.

Answers

The strongest answer:

(A) Money *talks*, and there's no doubt about it. Or as one person observed, "Those who believe money can do everything are frequently prepared to do everything for money." (Author unknown.)

The adequate answer:

(C) Gaining something for practically nothing is appealing, and so too is the possibility of money placed in the coffers at some future date. The bird-in-the-hand reward, however, is usually more persuasive.

The weakest answer:

(B) Too few people will benefit directly from this plan.

Rate yourself: Which one do you favor?

If you chose answer (A), give yourself 5 points.

If you chose answer (B), give yourself 1 point.

If you chose answer (C), give yourself 4 points.

Points earned: _____

The advertising director's options put the spotlight on two Presentation Skills:
1. **Offer monetary compensation.** The sum must be sufficient, and usually recipients want to justify taking the money.
2. **Gain acceptance from a group.** Group compliance tends to be impersonal and may be easier to obtain. When a group says yes, the onus is not on one person. Reluctant members of the group can put the blame on others and excuse themselves.

Question 6

Bill Weeks, an airplane pilot, stays in touch with a large part of the Phoenix, Arizona, business community via e-mail. The goodwill he generates often earns him an invitation to lunch or for drinks. Although the invitations are business-related, they could be confused with a social meeting. Bill's intention is to attract business and chase away the competition. When he keeps the appointment, he is always well prepared.

Which of the following is the best approach for getting the most out of casual meetings?

(A) Discussing a recent flight, Bill mentions benefits people might not think of themselves. "If my client flew with a large commercial air carrier, he'd have to fight traffic to get across town. I land the plane at the municipal airport. It's conveniently located, and we save time coming and going." And: "One of my clients is a cat, a company mascot who appears in commercials. Airline carriers charge about $160 round-trip for a cat. Private flight accommodates the cat without additional charges, and the cat travels with all the comforts of home."

(B) Bill maintains notes with personal references. Before a meeting, he refreshes his memory regarding a spouse's name, children's ages, and similar information. He works at building relationships and feels that business will result.

(C) Bill is consciously aware of letting the other person *lead* the conversation. If they want to talk about football, for instance, he's ready to talk about football. He's well informed about tennis, golf, world events, and more. He subscribes to a potpourri of magazines and reads them. Bill treats his "education" as necessary to business success.

Answers

The strongest answer:

(C) Bill is probably an outgoing person. That's one reason he values relationship building. Outgoing or extroverted people usually have so much to contribute to a conversation that it takes discipline to let others take the lead. Who could argue with the overall value of being well informed? In Bill's case, however, it's imperative because it prepares him to participate and makes him appear sincere.

The adequate answer:

(B) If your comments are not intrusive or contrived, people are usually pleased when you make thoughtful references to their family members.

The weakest answer:

(A) People might think you'll talk about them if you reveal sensitive information about other people. You'll want to be careful about how you "couch" benefits.

Rate yourself: Which one do you favor?

If you chose answer (A), give yourself 2 points.

If you chose answer (B), give yourself 4 points.

If you chose answer (C), give yourself 5 points.

Points earned: _____

Bill demonstrates these two important Presentation Skills:
1. **Know your topic.** It's said that knowledge is power. By staying well informed, you'll be able to counter objections, suggest remedies, and move in new directions as circumstances dictate.
2. **Think the way the birds think.** What do listeners want? Let them have it!

Question 7

Sedona uses a microphone properly, while her coworker Cliff is "microphone phobic." When he steps up to a microphone, it squeals, makes his voice sound like an echo, or otherwise "revolts." Cliff always blames the microphone.

Which of the following is the best approach for using a microphone?

(A) If it comes with instructions, read them.

(B) Practice before the audience arrives. Consult the "sound team" if you're having problems.

(C) Have someone sit at the far end of the room so he or she can tell you if you can be heard.

Answers

The strongest answer:

(A) Many speakers own microphones. Surely they can and should read instructions and follow them. But if you don't own the microphone, obtain instructions from a microphone manufacturer and read them. Many of the tips and suggestions offered will work with any microphone. (For example, go to www. google.com or www.dogpile.com and use key words: *microphone use* or *using a microphone.*)

The adequate answer:

(B) It's not always possible to "test" a microphone first. Sometimes you're not the first speaker and the audience is already seated and waiting for you. If possible, however, test it.

The weakest answer:

(C) You want to be sure you're being heard, but you'll have difficulty seeing someone sitting in the rear of a large room who might try to signal you. So if you have doubts about being heard, ask; "Is everyone able to hear me?"

Rate yourself: Which one do you favor?

If you chose answer **(A)**, give yourself 5 points.

If you chose answer **(B)**, give yourself 4 points.

If you chose answer **(C)**, give yourself 1 point.

Points earned: _____

When giving a speech or making any presentation with a microphone, consider the following:
- A microphone amplifies sound. It can't add emotion or variation or affect pace. Only you can do that.
- *Sound checks* let the speaker know all is well.

Question 8

Ray worried that he would forget what he was supposed to say when he had to speak to a group. He memorized everything but *sweated* through each presentation. He asked a coworker who was a confident speaker for some advice. "I cut out a circle of paper and divide it into segments," the coworker told him. "I jot my speech opening, middle, and closing on separate segments. Then I write key words and phrases in each segment. I make copies of this circle. I keep one in my pocket, one in a briefcase, and usually have one folded up and taped onto my cell phone. It's almost impossible to misplace or forget to take the paper with me. That's it. It's the secret to success."

Will this strategy work for others?

   (A) Self-confidence can be seen and heard! Do what you can to convince yourself you'll remember what you must say to an audience, and you'll put yourself into a veritable winner's circle.

   (B) Everyone must find a strategy that works well for him or her. It's important to test new methods before you depend upon them.

   (C) There's such a thing as overkill. Ray's coworker should be focused on more than remembering the speech.

Answers

The strongest answer:

(A) Who would argue with the value of self-confidence? The "circle divided into segments" strategy is inspired. Some well-known speakers use it too. Another way to build self-confidence is via positive self-talk: "I can do this!" And with those notes on hand, you'll have the support you need to believe what you tell yourself!

The adequate answer:

(B) Using trial and error methods may seem sensible, but take care not to expect "error." A positive approach to speaking and reliance upon techniques that help you do a great job are preferable. If you're convinced a tactic is worth trying, you should expect it to work. Period.

The weakest answer:

(C) Building self-confidence is an ongoing pursuit. The concept of "overkill" isn't applicable. The only reason this statement deserves even half a point is because no one thing will permit you to make admirable presentations. You may, for example, be self-confident, but if your speech doesn't flow in a logical manner, listeners will be none the better for having listened.

Rate yourself: Which one do you favor?

If you chose answer (A), give yourself 5 points.

If you chose answer (B), give yourself 4 points.

If you chose answer (C), give yourself ½ point.

Points earned: _____

The featured presentation skill is:
Sharpen self-confidence.

Question 9

The company's beloved star salesman died unexpectedly when he was out of the country conducting business. It took several weeks to arrange for his body to be flown back to Arizona. By then, employees' emotions were truly raw. When the salesman's widow announced that there would be a private graveside service, several managers approached the regional supervisor to ask him to conduct a memorial service at headquarters so employees could pay their respects and achieve closure. The supervisor didn't want to act in a manner contrary to the widow's plans, but he realized employees were grieving too. "What should I say to them?" he anguished.

Which of the following is best when your presentation must calm a group?

(A) The regional supervisor knew the deceased salesman well. He focused on how the loss affected everyone in the company: "I know I speak for everyone when I say that Ronald Harper will be missed by the many people who knew him well at LPO." The supervisor repeated complimentary things others said about Harper. He told about community service awards he received and reminded everyone of Harper's outspoken remarks to anyone who was insensitive to the special needs of the physically handicapped. He arranged for an organist to play soothing background music. When employees filed out of the room, he stood at the exit and shook their hands.

(B) The supervisor introduced a psychologist to the employees. "Dr. Graham will talk about grieving. Anyone who wants to speak with her privately may sign up for an appointment." Dr. Graham, who didn't know Ronald Harper, spoke in general terms. People filed out of the room quickly when she finished speaking.

(C) The regional supervisor gathered everyone together and announced there would be a few minutes of silence to honor Ronald Harper. He invited employees to make contributions to one of Harper's favorite charities. He arranged for light refreshments to be served and gave people a chance to mix and mingle. Later, he shook hands with employees as they exited.

Answers

The strongest answer:

(A) Since the regional supervisor had known the deceased, he was able to be specific and listeners could relate to his statements. He took time to shake hands with people. Some experts insist that "touch" (as in the handshake) has soothing powers. Music soothes too. This presentation was purposely built around touch, music, and words.

The adequate answer:

(C) The mixing/mingling opportunity was useful. It gave people a platform to talk and share thoughts. Someone, however, should have spoken for at least 10 minutes to the audience, and it should have been a high-ranking executive—probably the regional supervisor.

The weakest answer:

(B) By arranging for a grief expert to speak, the supervisor put people in an awkward position. This would be an extreme response. In addition, some employees might even feel guilty because they weren't grieving.

Rate yourself: Which one do you favor?

If you chose answer (A), give yourself 5 points.

If you chose answer (B), give yourself 1 point.

If you chose answer (C), give yourself 2 points.

Points earned: _____

The regional supervisor invoked the following Presentation Skills:
1. Offer well-known facts to all assembled.
2. Embrace the subtleties of body language.
3. Appeal to the senses.

Question 10

The Chamber of Commerce's Fifth Annual Awards Ceremony was scheduled for June 12, and the mayor was asked to do the honors. He was accustomed to making political speeches and handling various presenting challenges but believed something different was required for this occasion. He spoke to the Chamber's director and requested that some professional entertainers share the stage with him. "The occasion calls for entertainment," he told him, "and that's not my forte."

What should you take into account when the occasion calls for entertainment?

(A) You don't have to be a singer, dancer, or stand-up comedian in order to entertain a crowd. The fact that you're asked to be the master or mistress of ceremonies tells you that someone believes you can do the job. Use your creativity and rise to the occasion.

(B) Be self-critical. Perhaps, as the mayor decided, you can appear in the program and make a contribution. But if you don't think you can do the job alone, opt out fast so appropriate arrangements can be made. When you participate, find out what the others will be doing so your portion of the presentation won't be repetitive.

(C) You can't be all things to all people. You may be a fine and fearless presenter, but if an entertainment venue isn't for you, don't accept it. You don't need to chide yourself for using good judgment!

Answers

The strongest answer:

(B) A presentation that should entertain is one of the more challenging types of presentations. Sharing the responsibility isn't the same thing as opting out. Opting out may be the practical way to ensure that everyone will have a good time. If you say yes, be ready to play a minor role.

The adequate answer:

(A) Conduct research to learn about the award recipients. Look for human interest items that relate to specific awards. If Samantha Jones will receive an award for starting a literacy program, for example, and she was able to read when she was three years old, weave that information into a story for the audience. Or assemble an entertaining slide program. Use it to buoy your presentation. Sometimes all you need is a little ingenuity and some follow-through, and voilà, you're an entertainer.

The weakest answer:

(C) Unless you have a time conflict or other challenge that makes presenting impossible, you should accept the invitation and do your best to succeed. Yet, (C) earns 4 points because if in your opinion it's best to decline this offer, colleagues are likely to applaud your judgment call! "If it is not right do not do it; if it is not true do not say it." (Marcus Aurelius, Roman emperor.)

Rate yourself: Which one do you favor?

If you chose answer (A), give yourself 4 points.

If you chose answer (B), give yourself 5 points.

If you chose answer (C), give yourself 4 points.

Points earned: _____

The following Presentation Skill stands out:
Look for more than one way to get the job done.

Know Your Audience

Who is listening?

These three little words form a question that begs to be answered. You can't move forward with any speech or presentation until you *Know your audience*. It's not practical to turn this into a major research project, but the more you know, the better. Here are some audience descriptions you'll want to consider:

- Friendly, pleasant, welcoming

- Neutral, unbiased, middle of the road

- Hostile, unfriendly, argumentative, in opposition to your position

- Well informed versus ill informed (on the topic you're spotlighting)

- Educational background (graduate school versus high school dropout and everything in between)

- Environment (big city versus small-town residents, cultural traditions, prevailing political preferences/alignments)

- Job descriptions: incomes (affluent versus modest)

This section of the presentation IQ test spotlights important ways to learn more about your audience.

Question 11

Joe was going to speak to coworkers who were concerned about pollution problems. A major television station had featured their company as one of five whose practices caused ill health to people who lived near the main plant. Joe spent the previous months working with scientists who refuted the television show claims. He had concrete evidence to demonstrate that the reporters had relied upon old information that was both out of date and incorrect.

Joe felt good about what he had to report, but he assumed he would be walking into a highly charged situation. He doubted that members of the audience would understand the scientific jargon he had become familiar with, and he assumed that because none of the workers earned a high income, they hadn't traveled far or had opportunities to expand their knowledge of worldly matters. When he'd mingled with some of these employees in the past, he found them more interested in local gossip and local high school football statistics than anything else.

How could Joe determine whether his assumptions were good ones?

(A) Obtain copies of the local newspaper and read them.

(B) Call the mayor's office and chat with an official who might be forthcoming. Call another person in town, such as a physician and ask him or her questions, too.

(C) Speak to executives who work at the main plant. Make it clear that he wants to have a good understanding of the audience so he can give audience members useful information and not bore them or waste their time.

Answers

The strongest answer:

(C) It's always smart to look in your own backyard first. When speaking to executives at the plant, it will be necessary to frame questions so they're unbiased. For example, "Are most workers well informed about world events?" may not be an easy question to answer, but it doesn't pose a problem either. "Do these people know anything about the outside world?" is offensive. The answer might be flippant: "We drop the moat every Friday!"

The adequate answer:

(A) You can learn many things about people by reading the newspapers they read, including advertisements and entertainment offerings and even the types of crimes committed in the area. Joe could be misled, however, if plant workers make up only a tiny percentage of the newspaper's subscribers.

The weakest answer:

(B) The mayor and other elected officials are likely to be less than candid about constituents. They'll probably be inclined to paint a rosy picture. A local physician will feel bound by privacy considerations. Ever since the Health Insurance Portability and Accountability Act of 1996, and other legislation, was enacted, many physicians are reluctant to make statements, especially if they think something they say could be considered disparaging. It's not worth the risk, so this person's cooperation is doubtful.

Rate yourself: Which one do you favor?

If you chose answer (A), give yourself 3 points.

If you chose answer (B), give yourself 2 points.

If you chose answer (C), give yourself 5 points.

Points earned: _____

Question 12

Should an out of town speaker arrive a day ahead of schedule to "eyeball" the town and be exposed to behaviors that stand out (e.g., quick to smile versus a wariness of strangers, shaking hands upon meeting or simply nodding)?

(A) If time permits, this is an excellent thing to do.

(B) Conducting research in or around the hotel or company may not provide useful information. Take a taxi ride and talk to the driver, or go to a shopping mall and watch people and how they interact with one another.

(C) Forget it. This is storybook thinking. Do your research before you arrive, and keep your powers of observation open when you get where you're going.

Answers

The strongest answer:

(B) The environment in which you find yourself may be so different
from your usual environment that you could mistakenly believe
it represents those who will be in your audience. Continue your
search for information about presentation attendees with a practical eye. If folks are quick with handshakes and smiles, that
behavior may prevail in the wider community, but if everyone at
the breakfast café is reading the *Wall Street Journal*, that may have
no bearing on what you can expect from your audience.

The adequate answer:

(A) It's not sufficient to arrive early for purposes of getting to know
your audience. Do your homework beforehand, but this can be a
time to add to that information. How you spend the extra hours
will greatly affect what you bring to the mix. If you travel from a
distant place, you'll minimize jet lag disturbances by presentation time and be better prepared to be observant.

The weakest answer:

(C) When you arrive, you'll be too busy for this quest. Other matters
will take priority (e.g., transportation to the site, meeting your
hosts, reviewing your speech). That may be why one would be
inclined to call this "storybook thinking." Still, there's no substitute for being there. You'll toss away a good opportunity to learn
more about your audience if you ignore all the little signs that are
in front of you.

Rate yourself: Which one do you favor?

If you chose answer **(A)**, give yourself 4 points.

If you chose answer (B), give yourself 5 points.

If you chose answer **(C)**, give yourself 3 points.

Points earned: _____

Question 13

How much technical language can you use when speaking to physicians or attorneys or others in highly specialized fields of work?

(A) The language you use depends greatly upon your topic. If you're speaking about new advances in medicine to a group of physicians, feel free to use technical language. If you're speaking to them about computer systems that make business operations efficient, you don't want to talk like a computer geek.

(B) Provide definitions and go for it! A group that has more formal education should catch on quickly.

(C) You'll want to be careful not to "talk down" to a crowd that's well educated. At the same time, you shouldn't talk down to anyone. A condescending or superior attitude will usually turn off listeners.

Answers

The strongest answer:

(C) When you speak, your attitude shows! An audience is like a finely tuned measuring device when it comes to recognizing that you like them or don't like them, care about them or don't care about them, etc. It's important that you say nothing to people that can be construed as disrespectful.

The adequate answer:

(A) It's true the language you use depends greatly upon your topic, but even then you must tie what you have to say carefully to benefits. You won't win over a crowd of insurance industry actuaries because you toss out accepted mathematical equations. Talk to them about how these equations shave company losses by 2 percent, and you'll have their rapt attention!

The weakest answer:

(B) There's no reason to deduce that aeronautical engineers will quickly master a vocabulary that's used by financial planners. You may assist any audience to become comfortable with unfamiliar terms by providing definitions. If, however, this isn't necessary to what you're trying to accomplish, it's a waste of time.

Rate yourself: Which one do you favor?

If you chose answer (A), give yourself 3 points.

If you chose answer (B), give yourself 0 points.

If you chose answer (C), give yourself 5 points.

Points earned: _____

"Too many people grow up. That's the real trouble with the world, too many people grow up. They forget. They don't remember what it's like to be 12 years old. They patronize, they treat children as inferiors. Well, I won't do that."
    Attributed to Walt Disney (1901–1966), pioneer of animated cartoon films.

Question 14

Donna, a 1998 college graduate, was invited to return to her alma mater to deliver a speech to a national women's group. She spoke frequently about successful women working in the fields of science and mathematics, and since she would be speaking to an audience on a campus she once called home, she spent little time on preparation.

Was Donna overly confident?

(A) Donna has every reason to believe she'll be well received by this audience. Furthermore, she has a good understanding of the kind of information she can offer that will benefit these people who attend her presentation.

(B) Changes come about rapidly, and if Donna hasn't been on this campus since 1998, she's more than five years behind the times. Does she think that students will be the only people in the audience? What does Donna know about the women's group? She should have asked more questions!

(C) Donna can wait until she arrives to put her finger on the proverbial pulse of this audience. She may have a "home" advantage, but she is still well advised to make a few inquiries. This audience has every reason to believe that "one of its own" will make time spent listening to her worthwhile.

Answers

The strongest answer:

(B) Speakers are easily lured into a comfort zone when they're in familiar territory, but it's essential for them to examine the full picture. Since Donna's audience will probably be composed of members of the women's group too, she should treat the audience analysis in the standard manner.

The adequate answer:

(C) Like it or not, it's never wise to assume you know your audience until you make inquiries about current circumstances. At the same time, give credit where credit is due. Donna should enjoy the prospect of speaking to the home team and should permit herself the luxury of a quick, rather than lengthy, probe into what's new.

The weakest answer:

(A) You can't provide the kind of information your audience needs and wants unless you know more about it. Donna may be well received because of advance publicity that refers to her as an accomplished alumna, but she risks disappointing attendees if she doesn't take time to update herself.

Rate yourself: Which one do you favor?

If you chose answer **(A)**, give yourself 1 point.

If you chose answer **(B)**, give yourself 5 points.

If you chose answer **(C)**, give yourself 4 points.

Points earned: _____

A "home advantage" is frequently mentioned in regard to teams winning competitions. It appears when people perform in familiar surroundings, they have an advantage.

Question 15

Fred travels widely to promote his company's products. He finds it easy to enter a room, shake hands with those assembled, and explain why he's there. Yet when his boss asked him to travel to Italy and make a formal presentation to investors, he froze. "I'm not a formal kind of guy," he told her. "And what do I know about Italy?"

What could the boss say to make him realize that he was just the person for the job?

(A) She could remind him that his natural ability had taken him quite far and now he had the opportunity to demonstrate to management that he was a serious contender for a leadership position and a bright future with the company.

(B) She may want to suggest that he join Toastmasters International. "You don't know how good you are," she praised him. "I'm a member of TM, and, if you join, I think you'll recognize that you're quite an accomplished speaker."

(C) She made him an offer that was hard to refuse: "Your trip to Italy will be all expenses paid, and that includes airfare for a companion. You can add three or four days for sightseeing,"

Answers

The strongest answer:

(C) It's likely that Fred's boss knows her audience, namely: Fred. She is making an offer that he finds appealing. It probably rates as number one in regard to what she can do to motivate him.

The adequate answer:

(B) Toastmasters International is devoted to assisting people in improving communication skills and helping them to "achieve their full potential and realize their dreams." It's easy to join.

The weakest answer:

(A) Fred may believe that management will ultimately recognize he's a productive and dedicated employee whether or not he travels to Italy to make a presentation. If he's fearful of speaking in the setting the boss suggests, he probably won't be comforted by these possibilities, though her argument has merit.

Rate yourself: Which one do you favor?

If you chose answer (A), give yourself 1 point.

If you chose answer (B), give yourself 4 points.

If you chose answer (C), give yourself 5 points.

Points earned: _____

Preparing to speak to people who live in other countries or come from different cultural backgrounds forces you to add steps to the *Know your audience* quest. Pick up brochures from a travel agent, surf the Web, or check out an encyclopedia in order to familiarize yourself with the country, people, and customs. Will you need the services of a translator? If you normally refer to well-known places in the United States to help make a point, provide different reference points for this new audience.

Question 16

Susan and Stuart instructed new lifeguards on how to administer cardio-pulmonary resuscitation (CPR). They scheduled brush-up CPR classes for lifeguards who returned to work summer after summer. All year round they operated a school for competitive swimmers and helped many qualify for the Olympics and other competitive events. They considered themselves excellent presenters. One day, however, they were stymied. Three men and three women were hired to fill new lifeguard positions. The women learned CPR quickly but the men didn't. How could Susan and Stuart find out why?

(A) Ask them. Susan and Stuart have the luxury of talking to each of the men, since it's such a small group. They should learn more about these men: what makes them tick (i.e., are they well spoken, curious, eager to please?) and why they're having difficulty with the class.

(B) Since Susan and Stuart don't teach at the same time, they should confer to find out if one is working differently from the other. Either Susan or Stuart may have tweaked his or her presentation and strayed too far from the original successful program.

(C) Susan and Stuart should chalk up the "failure" to hiring people who are slow learners. Since CPR proficiency is necessary for all lifeguards, give these new hires other jobs.

Answers

The strongest answer:

(C) Susan and Stuart always bring high standards and integrity to their work. As tenacious as we should all be about doing a job right, sometimes no matter what you do, you can't meet goals. It's very important for a speaker to admit to a "can't win them all" scenario. Failing to do so will disembowel the speaker. If that happens, everyone loses.

The adequate answer:

(A) This approach represents taking action "after the fact." Most presenters don't get a second chance. There's no reason why Susan and Stuart can't take this approach, but they'll have to be excellent detectives since the men may not be forthcoming about their concerns.

The weakest answer:

(B) The spotlight should be on *Know your audience*. Still, a presenter should never be so married to one method of maintaining excellence that he or she isn't willing to step outside the box. Save this assessment for last and plan to use it if necessary. It shouldn't take more than a few minutes to spot possible glitches in presentations that once served needs admirably.

Rate yourself: Which one do you favor?

If you chose answer **(A)**, give yourself 2 points.

If you chose answer **(B)**, give yourself 1 point.

If you chose answer **(C)**, give yourself 5 points.

Points earned: _____

It's often said that "two heads are better than one." Seek assistance from another "head" when one is available!

Question 17

Susan is a public information officer accustomed to speaking to journalists at press conferences. She often says, "I know what journalists want, and I deliver!" To judge from the great number of positive stories her agency receives, you can't argue with her. There are five items that appear on Susan's press conference "must do" list in no particular order of importance:

- Don't hold a press conference on a Monday.

- Speak in the morning and keep it short—no more than one hour.

- Don't expect journalists to travel far to listen to you—you or your officials may have to do the traveling.

- Accommodate TV crews with sufficient space to set up cameras, and make sure there's easy access to electrical outlets.

- Send a messenger to deliver press kits to reporters who couldn't attend but will probably cover the story.

Which should be at the top of the list and why?

    (A) Avoid Mondays and favor mornings. That's because the working press has scheduling preferences and deadlines to meet. In most offices, Mondays are devoted to paperwork. Of course, you'll want to see if that applies to journalists with whom you interact.

    (B) Susan left out the most important thing: Call a press conference only when there's something of great importance to impart to reporters and there's no better way to do it. If you're not judicious about calling conferences, journalists will remember. Conference room chairs will be empty the next time you call one.

    (C) Choose a meeting place that's centrally located and easy to access. Send press kits to no-shows in a timely fashion.

Answers

The strongest answer:

(B) Is the story newsworthy and timely? Will key officials or experts be available to answer questions? Can you inform media effectively without calling a press conference? These questions deserve top billing. It won't matter, for example, if your press kits are dazzling and delivered to all interested parties if the story isn't newsworthy and timely.

The adequate answer:

(A) Knowing when the best time is to call a conference demonstrates consideration for journalists who attend. Since you work with these people over and over again, it's a smart step. Still, it isn't a priority item. If, for example, there's a warehouse fire at 3:00 P.M. and densely populated neighborhoods are evacuated, the fire chief won't (and shouldn't) wait until Tuesday or the next morning to hold a press conference.

The weakest answer:

(C) You can't always choose the meeting place. So, although it deserves a place on the "must do" press conference list, it belongs at the bottom. It may be a waste of time and dollars to send press kits to no-shows. This action shouldn't be automatic. Determine this case by case each time you call a press conference.

Rate yourself: Which one do you favor?

If you chose answer (A), give yourself 4 points.

If you chose answer (B), give yourself 5 points.

If you chose answer (C), give yourself 2 points.

Points earned: _____

A press conference is also known as a "news conference."

Question 18

Lindsey was on stage speaking when she realized she was getting blank stares from the members of the audience. She stopped speaking, walked to the edge of the stage, and asked people sitting in the front row whether something was wrong. One man answered, "Most of us speak Spanish." Lindsey apologized to the group in Spanish even though she couldn't speak the language well. They applauded her efforts to speak their language but the presentation was over.

How could Lindsey have avoided this embarrassment?

(A) She should have asked, "Can anyone in the audience speak both English and Spanish, and if so, are you willing to assist me?" If someone stepped forward, she could have used this assistant to sum up quickly and end the program. It would have afforded a more gracious and better way to conclude the event.

(B) She should have done a much better job with her *Know your audience* preparation. Still, the "unexpected" can arise, and a speaker should "think on his or her feet."

(C) Lindsey couldn't do anything about the clumsy end to the presentation but could follow up by contacting attendees with a formal letter of apology. It's rude to waste people's time and courteous to let them know you feel this way. Can she give them something of value too? If, for example, this is a group that meets regularly, she may want to supply cake or refreshments at a future gathering. It would speak well of her if she didn't simply dash off and disappear.

Answers

The strongest answer:

(B) It's difficult to overlook the fact that your listeners don't speak your language. Obviously, this was a major faux pas. At the same time, speakers can be confronted with a host of things they didn't or couldn't know ahead of time. Think about the people who have come to listen to you. How can you make things better for them? Answer that question and move on.

The adequate answer:

(A) Lindsey was quick to realize something was wrong, and that speaks well for monitoring audience response. She probably would have left the group with a better impression if she had enlisted the aid of someone in the audience to apologize and present some useful information. For example, she could have informed an audience gathered to learn more about the community's year long schedule of road construction to read page two of the *Daily Record* on, Wednesdays, or whenever current road closings or detours are listed: information that she knows is regularly printed in Spanish as well as English.

The weakest answer:

(C) There's nothing wrong with trying to make amends, but people may not even remember your name one month from now.

Rate yourself: Which one do you favor?

If you chose answer **(A)**, give yourself 4 points.

If you chose answer **(B)**, give yourself 5 points.

If you chose answer **(C)**, give yourself 1 point.

Points earned: _____

As Mario Andretti, legendary race car driver, put it: "If everything is under control, you're going too slow."

Question 19

Kevin enjoyed speaking to groups of hikers. These presentations were part of his job as a park ranger. People were friendly and the atmosphere relaxed. Although he had to impress audiences with the need for safety, each event was usually both leisurely and casual. One day Kevin received a notice from his new boss: "I have been in the audience at recent presentations. I think your gatherings generate goodwill with visitors but you don't achieve goals. Please read and follow the attached instructions. Someone from my office will attend many of your presentations over the next few months. Let's try to do better."

How should Kevin respond?

(A) Read and follow instructions. Take notes about whether the new directions help or hinder him. Be ready to discuss details with the boss.

(B) Ask for a meeting with his boss. Ask for more input so he knows what the boss perceives as inappropriate. Let the boss know that he has drawers filled with thank-you letters from visitors who attended his programs. Let the boss know that hiking accidents have decreased by 5 percent since he began giving these presentations.

(C) Ask a coworker to sit in on a presentation and critique his performance. Tell that person to list anything that might need improvement. Then read the instructions the boss sent. See if the coworker flagged items that are also mentioned in the instructions. If so, concentrate on improvement in those areas first.

Answers

The strongest answer:

(B) Measurement is the "darling" of communication professionals. "Without measurement, how can we demonstrate our value?" they query. The letters Kevin saved and statistics he can show validate how well he's doing with his presentations. It appears he knows his audience! The boss should receive this information pronto. It establishes a baseline against which to measure future performance. The boss and his new instructions will be put to the test too. If it can be demonstrated that change improves results, Kevin will probably embrace change effortlessly.

The adequate answer:

(C) Kevin is probably too subjective to evaluate himself. He should take pains to assure his colleague that he's open to constructive criticism. Since he makes presentations on an ongoing basis, he should move ahead to make changes in areas that automatically "float to the top."

The weakest answer:

(A) Kevin is probably uncomfortable with the notion that he's being watched. Before working on new instructions, he'd be well advised to speak with his boss. A two-way conversation should help establish a comfort zone and free him to get on with his work.

Rate yourself: Which one do you favor?

If you chose answer **(A)** give yourself 2 points.

If you chose answer **(B)**, give yourself 5 points.

If you chose answer **(C)**, give yourself 3 points.

Points earned: _____

Question 20

Augusta was scheduled to meet with the CEO of a major company. She was a ghostwriter, and sometimes people thought her fee for services was excessive. "You can buy a fancy new car for that money," she'd been told. She knew that the fee for the service she would present was fair. Moreover, she could do an excellent job.

What should Augusta do to counter the comment that her ghostwriting services are too expensive before it is made?

(A) It doesn't matter if Augusta's fee for service is fair if the CEO can't afford her services. She should *qualify* her before she takes times to prepare her oral presentation and meet with the woman.

(B) She should let a potential client know the work will take many months to complete. She should explain that she will be working exclusively on one book manuscript during that period. If she asks for $25,000 for a job that will take four months to complete, the listener can do the math. If that person thinks ghostwriters deserve to earn upward of $75,000 a year, Augusta shouldn't hear complaints about her fee. She can proceed with her proposal once that's out of the way.

(C) Augusta shouldn't be concerned about whether the CEO can afford her services. She should move ahead with her presentation and focus on how her services will benefit the CEO. She'll refer to her expertise, credits, achievements, successes, and experience. If she begins by making excuses or lingers too long on apologetic explanations, she'll be defeated before she begins. Savvy individuals know that the cost of this kind of service will be comparable to buying great advertising, and that's never cheap.

Answers

The strongest answer:

(B) It's not every day that a person hires a ghostwriter, so it's not surprising when people have no idea of the cost involved. Even when they know Augusta is one of the best in her field, she should take the time to demonstrate that her yearly wages are reasonable and therefore her fee for service is appropriate.

The adequate answer:

(C) When making a proposal, one shouldn't be too concerned about revealing information (e.g., fee structure) that listeners may be unprepared to receive. People should feel fortunate to have been introduced to Augusta, and everything she tells them should make them realize it.

The weakest answer:

(A) You can find out many things about an audience before you appear in front of it, but you may not be able to ascertain the budget for your services. Theoretically this is an ideal approach, but realistically Augusta probably can't qualify the audience with any accuracy.

Rate yourself: Which one do you favor?

If you chose answer (A), give yourself 2 points.

If you chose answer (B), give yourself 5 points.

If you chose answer (C), give yourself 3 points.

Points earned: _____

Beginnings, Middles, and Ends

Organizing Your Presentation

A presentation typically has three parts: the beginning, middle, and end. Excellent presentations usually result when each of these parts is carefully prepared. The questions in this section of the Presentation IQ Test are designed to spotlight priorities and demonstrate the good, better, and best ways to analyze and organize a presentation.

Question 21

Do you need to prepare for more or fewer than three parts to a presentation?

    (A) It is possible to develop the middle part of a speech in sections. Components would eventually be combined and represent the middle of the presentation.

    (B) There's always a beginning, so get that in place and just wing the rest.

    (C) As long as you make your points, you don't really need a formal ending.

Answers

The strongest answer:

(A) If your presentation is long or even if you must make several short points, you may want to prepare the middle, or the body of the speech, in sections. For example, Ellen had to update the Customer Service staff about benefits related to three new products. She prepared by focusing on one product at a time. But the middle of her presentation included benefits that each product delivered. In this case, Ellen prepared her speech as though it contained five parts. There was a beginning, a three-pronged middle, and an end.

The adequate answer:

(B) It is true that there's always a beginning. Still, if you prepare only your opening remarks, no matter how provocative they are, where will you go from there? Admittedly, some people can "wing it." They're excellent extemporaneous speakers, and after they get a jump start they're ready to fly. This state of euphoria usually comes to a thoroughly topic-knowledgeable speaker.

The weakest answer:

(C) Sometimes there isn't a discernable end to a presentation. A speaker may say, "Thanks for listening," or use words to that affect as he or she exits, but one could argue whether that's an appropriate end. If comments are made that could be said at the close of any presentation, it's probable that the speaker didn't prepare an end. That speaker forfeits the opportunity to provide listeners with a powerful finale.

Rate yourself: Which one do you favor?

If you chose answer (A), give yourself 5 points.

If you chose answer (B), give yourself 3 points.

If you chose answer (C), give yourself ½ point.

Points earned: _____

Question 22

Should speakers always ask the audience questions?

(A) The question the speaker asks should relate to the topic under discussion. Otherwise interest is likely to fade when he or she delivers the middle of the speech, even when people in the audience supplied answers to the question.

(B) Questions that grab attention help introduce a presentation. It's possible to introduce a question, however, without asking the audience to supply an answer. The speaker can promise to answer the question as the presentation unfolds or can offer multiple-choice answers to whet appetites.

(C) Even lackluster questions (e.g., "How many people are from Indiana?") are better than no questions at all.

Answers

The strongest answer:

(A) People often like to answer questions or to discover if they have the best answers to questions. As a result, if you open your remarks with a well-planned question, you're in a strong position to draw attention, whether listeners answer aloud or not.

The adequate answer:

(B) No one can argue with the merit of this observation. Still, a question and answer session at the start of a presentation may serve to warm up the audience. Or it may relax people or help set a mood even though the questions don't relate closely to what comes next.

The weakest answer:

(C) It's possible to successfully open a presentation with a quotation, a fact, or a short story, and you may not want to ask a question. But if you do, try to come up with one that sparks interest.

Rate yourself: Which one do you favor?

If you chose answer (A), give yourself 5 points.

If you chose answer (B), give yourself 4 points.

If you chose answer (C), give yourself zero points.

Points earned: _____

When many people hear a question, they start to think about an answer. Then they wonder if the answers are correct. If you provide an answer that is very different from the one most people supplied, they may question your credibility. In short, a question tends to start a chain reaction of thought and involvement, and that's why an exciting question can be most effective when you make a speech or otherwise get things started.

Question 23

Does the middle of a presentation need three or more supporting facts or figures to back up the opening remarks?

(A) There's no need to mention facts and figures when you can distribute handouts to your listeners.

(B) It follows that you'll want to back up opening remarks with supporting evidence. If you don't, there's a good chance your listeners won't come to the conclusions you want them to reach.

(C) When you're new at making presentations, you may want to adopt this axiom: "Offer at least three supporting facts or figures to the listeners."

Answers

The strongest answer:

(B) Well-documented facts and figures are difficult to ignore or refute. Still, you may be able to rely upon consensus too. If, for example, you ask for a "show of hands" regarding a topic and receive an overwhelming response, this serves to support assertions.

The adequate answer:

(C) Some speakers find it easier to prepare a presentation when they follow an exact plan. Seasoned speakers are likely to want more latitude and make decisions regarding supporting material as needs arise.

The weakest answer:

(A) It may be risky to rely solely upon a handout to deliver information that supports your assertions. People may not read it before you bring your presentation to a conclusion. If you're hoping to conclude by winning over the audience, this omission could be your Achilles' heel.

Rate yourself: Which one do you favor?

If you chose answer **(A)**, give yourself zero points.

If you chose answer **(B)**, give yourself 5 points.

If you chose answer **(C)**, give yourself 3 points.

Points earned: _____

Earlier in the book various types of presentations are discussed. These include: reporting, informing, explaining, announcing, and persuading. It's difficult to do any of these things without offering facts or figures. Not only should you be prepared with sufficient material, but it should be well researched and up-to-date. It would be a mistake to quote old figures or rely upon information that has been discredited.

Question 24

Should the end of your presentation always be "a call to action"?

(A) It's almost always appropriate to restate main points briefly. But whether or not you end with a "call to action" depends upon the type of presentation you deliver.

For example, when Kevin updated regional sales personnel on new warehouse locations, shipping options, and related costs, a call to action didn't apply. At another meeting he urged sales personnel to make better use of interactive warehouse computer programs. This presentation ended with a strong request: Use these programs!

(B) As you conclude your presentation, assign yourself a call to action. Review your performance and plan to take specific steps to make improvements. Since perfection is essentially a notion, there's always something you can improve upon.

(C) Even when you introduce a speaker or disseminate information to the media, you conclude with some kind of "call to action." You want listeners to gain something, even if the something is the retention of new information.

Answers

The strongest answer:

(A) It's true that the purpose of your presentation dictates whether you close with "a call to action." But even when you don't, plan to end with an exciting summary or use vivid word pictures to wrap up. Otherwise, folks may be gathering papers, looking for car keys, or be distracted by other concerns. Your comments should *be good to the last drop*.

The adequate answer:

(C) You anticipate that listeners will be changed in some way when your presentation concludes. That's reasonable. But you'll probably enjoy more success when you reserve "call to action" endings for overt action times. "Get out and vote!" "Reserve vacation time today!" "Sign up for the Stop Smoking clinic now!"

The weakest answer:

(B) You must focus on your speech and your audience from start to finish, and that doesn't leave room for you to ask, "How am I doing?" Wait until the presentation is over and people leave the room (or you leave the room) before beginning a self-examination.

Rate yourself: Which one do you favor?

If you chose answer (A), give yourself 5 points.

If you chose answer (B), give yourself zero points.

If you chose answer (C), give yourself 3 points.

Points earned: _____

A presentation's conclusion is akin to marching orders. In other words, you're getting ready to dismiss the listeners. Give them something valuable to remember you by.

Question 25

Is it useful to quote famous people even if my listeners don't know the people I quote?

(A) Quotes are valuable, especially when they deliver a message in a creative way. If you think your audience won't know the person you're quoting, add a few words of explanation: "She was a historian and an author." "He is a baseball player."

(B) Challenge yourself to find quotes that are attributed to people most of your listeners will know. You may be thoroughly familiar with auto racing, for example, and think everyone knows the racing greats, but an audience filled with ballet buffs isn't likely to have a clue.

(C) Rely upon quotes from company executives or others in the community, such as the mayor.

Answers

The strongest answer:

(A) You're wise not to assume that a person you're quoting is familiar to everyone in your audience. A few words of explanation are almost always in order. The quote has more relevance when the person is known. That's because we're predisposed to embrace comments about achieving success that are made by someone who is successful, to embrace comments about hard work made by someone who works hard, and so on.

The adequate answer:

(B) Since the Internet and other quick reference channels make quotations readily available, it may be easy for you to quote people to whom your audience is likely to relate. However, this shouldn't be the priority; a dead-on quote should be the priority.

The weakest answer:

(C) You narrow your focus too much when you limit your search for appropriate quotations to company and community figures. Also, your listeners may have diverse opinions about these individuals, in which case, if they don't like or agree with the person you quote, the quote works against you.

Rate yourself: Which one do you favor?

If you chose answer (A), give yourself 5 points.

If you chose answer (B), give yourself 4 points.

If you chose answer (C), give yourself 1 point.

Points earned: _____

People tend to respond favorably to comments made by respected, popular people. When you quote those individuals, it's as though they're aligned with you. *We're frequently judged by the company we keep*!

Question 26

I think of my introduction to the group as the beginning of my presentation. Would you agree?

    (A) It's not my responsibility to introduce myself to the group. That job belongs to the hosting organization. I concentrate on preparing my opening remarks.

    (B) The audience should know something about you and why its members should listen to you. Even if you're "the boss," it can't hurt to offer details that support your expertise (e.g., "We used this approach for the three years I supervised operations at Dallas headquarters"). When someone else introduces you to a group, make sure that person has relevant information.

    (C) An introduction is not truly the beginning of a speech. It is set apart. Steve usually spoke to groups about crime victims' rights and entitlements. It was useful for listeners to know that Steve is an attorney. In the introduction, the audience also learned how many years of experience he had in this specialty.

Answers

The strongest answer:

(C) What the audience knows about you lends credence to what you want to tell them. If a person who introduces you doesn't do it for you, do it yourself. Ideally, you would supply your host with a written script. If you're fortunate, the person will use it. Focus on aspects of your background that relate to your topic. This is no time for modesty. When you prepare the beginning portion of your speech, it may be necessary to take care of this chore. Be ready.

The adequate answer:

(A) Strictly speaking, an introduction isn't the same as the beginning of your speech or presentation. It may be, however, that you have to *think on your feet* and introduce yourself. A long pause can serve as a line of demarcation. Consider making a long pause before delivering the beginning of your speech.

The weakest answer:

(B) This view is shortsighted. If you're an astronaut and talk about going to the moon but no one knows that you're an astronaut, how will your comments be received?

Rate yourself: Which one do you favor?

If you chose answer (A), give yourself 3 points.

If you chose answer (B), give yourself zero points.

If you chose answer (C), give yourself 5 points.

Points earned: _____

Introductions that work in your favor deserve your careful attention. A confident speaker might mail the introduction to the host prior to the day of the presentation. Then she brings a copy of it to a meeting just in case it's needed.

Question 27

Would you agree that after taking the time and care needed to prepare my remarks (beginning, middle, end), I'll remember them and don't need to practice?

(A) A thorough familiarity with your material is commendable, but it makes sense to have a few notes available for quick reference. Practice without referring to them. If you must glance at notes, practice doing so in an unobtrusive manner.

(B) Careful preparation of your program is likely to build confidence, but that's not *the whole ballgame*. Your delivery needs practice. Vocal pitch and pace and body language need to be finely honed.

(C) There is such a thing as too much practice. Since I'm a good speaker and prepare my speech well, I don't have to practice.

Answers

The strongest answer:

(B) Think of a stirring presentation you watched someone deliver. What would happen if he or she made the presentation in a monotone or spoke too quickly or loudly? The speaker who invests time in practicing the delivery isn't likely to disappoint or to be disappointed.

The adequate answer:

(A) How would you feel if someone read a presentation to you? It's likely you'd want to leave the room. After all, you can read to yourself; you don't need someone to do it for you. So don't read to your listeners, but be practical: If you get distracted, your audience will be better served when you have excellent notes at the ready. Refer to them briefly and move on.

The weakest answer:

(C) Too much practice is akin to too much happiness. It's difficult to imagine too much of either one. Of course, if you become obsessive about a presentation and neglect other responsibilities, that's worrisome.

Rate yourself: Which one do you favor?

If you chose answer **(A)**, give yourself 4 points.

If you chose answer **(B)**, give yourself 5 points.

If you chose answer **(C)**, give yourself 1 point.

Points earned: _____

Prior to a speaking engagement, think about what you'll say and how you'll say it, but don't ignore the big picture. If you don't have a checklist, you may want to create one. And when possible, scrutinize fine points: Is the microphone operating efficiently? Et cetera.

Question 28

Is it best to end a presentation on a humorous note?

    (A) When possible, always leave them laughing!

    (B) Not when your message is a serious one.

    (C) Don't bother if you can't tell a joke well.

Answers

The strongest answer:

(A) Laughter can serve as a memory jog. Use this knowledge to your advantage if you can. Dave was fond of telling listeners some of the funny things children said about tongue depressors and eye charts. It's likely anyone who heard him speak would remember he's a pediatrician.

The adequate answer:

(B) Some people may think you lack good judgment when you end with humor after speaking on a solemn topic. But others would be relieved to have something to smile about. Before you make this decision, consider the makeup of your audience. If in doubt, leave it out.

The weakest answer:

(C) Humor is a valuable communication tool and you may not take advantage of it if you take a defeatist attitude. At the same time, you'll want to avoid delivering a "botched" ending.

Rate yourself: Which one do you favor?

If you chose answer (A), give yourself 5 points.

If you chose answer (B), give yourself 3 points.

If you chose answer (C), give yourself 2 points.

Points earned: _____

People weren't born telling humorous stories or jokes. It's an acquired skill, and though some people have a knack for finding humor in most things, it's likely that most people can find humor in some things. Take baby steps, if you must, but try using humor when you make presentations. Leave them laughing when you can and pay attention to the results.

Question 29

Some presentations extend over a period of time. Webinars (workshops presented electronically on the Internet.), for example, can last for weeks, with a new module posted every Wednesday. If I'm asked to present a Webinar, do I prepare a beginning, middle, and end?

(A) Yes. Unlike other presentations, Webinars are usually archived. A participant can reference earlier presentations. Still, you need to present Webinars in a logical order, and the beginning, middle, end approach is successful.

(B) Treat each presentation as new and unrelated to earlier presentations. Even though you develop a beginning, middle, and end, don't feel tied to what has come before.

(C) When any program continues for more than one session, participants should have a syllabus. Whether you address the group in real time or face to face, or your presentation begins when the participant logs in at his or her convenience, a beginning, middle, end approach works.

Answers

The strongest answer:

(A) Since a Webinar is a major production, an excellent outline will enable you to "get your arms around" the project. Each module you place in the outline will have components that fit into beginning, middle, and end categories. Participants will find archived modules are related and therefore more useful.

The adequate answer:

(C) Attendees of interrupted programs are likely to benefit when a visual map is at their disposal. But when the program is presented in real time, a speaker can offer a brief review when each session gets under way. This could take the place of written documentation.

The weakest answer:

(B) Each presentation may be new, but it is related to what came before and what may come later. Remember this when you prepare segments, or you risk not achieving your goal.

Rate yourself: Which one do you favor?

If you chose answer (A), give yourself 5 points.

If you chose answer (B), give yourself zero points.

If you chose answer (C), give yourself 3 points.

Points earned: _____

Ongoing presentations interrupted by hours, days, or weeks require speakers to "connect" components. It's difficult to think of a better way to do it than using beginning, middle, and end preparation guidelines. Remember, electronic presentations offer new opportunities. You can direct your audience to Web links to obtain enhancement data, and you can conduct interactive training.

Question 30

How useful is the advice: "Tell them what you're going to tell them. Tell them. Tell them what you told them"?

(A) Mary, a professional trainer, doesn't like this approach. "When I think of my presentation this way, it seems unnatural. I prefer to use only the last piece of this advice. I always provide a summary."

(B) This is the quintessential beginning, middle, and end. Take apart any worthwhile presentation and you'll find these components, even if they are somewhat disguised.

(C) This well-traveled advice reminds us that people work hard to be good communicators, albeit using varied approaches. For example, Corrine is an artist, and when she plans a presentation, she says she "thinks in colors":

> "I start out bright; make a promise or deliver information that is new and exciting. I use easy-to-look-at hues in the middle while delivering logical information. I paint with bright colors as I close. I want people to be excited about what they've learned, and think about it as they leave."

Answers

The strongest answer:

(B) How can we describe the presentation process better? Even when you see a movie, someone tells you what to expect (that's probably why you decide in favor of attending one movie rather than another). Of course, the beginning of the movie "tells" you something too. As the film progresses information is delivered—that's the "tell them" component. At the conclusion, if you don't walk out with what you've been told to expect or a satisfying version of it, the experience isn't satisfactory. It's likely to be quickly forgotten.

The adequate answer:

(C) Make the most of information you can apply with ease, but don't be reluctant to try new ways of arranging your presentations. Everything you do was new once. Keep your pioneer spirit alive and be willing to try things.

The weakest answer:

(A) The fact that Mary doesn't like the approach doesn't diminish its value.

Rate yourself: Which one do you favor?

If you chose answer (A), give yourself 1 point.

If you chose answer (B), give yourself 5 points.

If you chose answer (C), give yourself 4 points.

Points earned: _____

As William R. Alger (1822–1905, American theologian) put it: "We give advice by the bucket, but take it by the grain."

Test Four

Using Visuals

Did you ever wish you had an assistant to help deliver a presentation? With visuals, you actually do. Effective visuals enable listeners to see as well as hear a message, thereby appealing to both right brain and left brain capabilities. (Note: The left brain is wired to listen, while the right brain excels at spatial and visual intake.) It follows that visuals engage the audience more fully in the communication process. Even though they should support statements and not duplicate them, they can double as notes, making it practically impossible for you to lose your place, to wander or forget.

The questions in this section of the Presentation IQ Test specifically concern the best ways to use visuals in various types of presentations.

Question 31

When should I use visuals?

- **(A)** I can always use them but especially when I'm talking to large groups of people.
- **(B)** There's such a thing as overkill. If everyone else dazzles listeners with visuals, I may want to forgo them. In short, no one-size answer fits all.
- **(C)** Always use them.

Answers

The strongest answer:

(A) It's almost never wrong to use visuals, but if you make a presentation on short notice or will speak to one or just a few people, you probably don't need to bother.

The adequate answer:

(B) It's important to think about your audience when you prepare a presentation, and it's possible members of the audience have been exposed to too much of a good thing. They may not pay attention to your visuals because they assume it's the same old, same old.

The weakest answer:

(C) No visuals are better than inadequate visuals. If you don't have excellent material to use, forget about it!

Rate yourself: Which one do you favor?

If you chose answer **(A)**, give yourself 5 points.

If you chose answer **(B)**, give yourself 3 points.

If you chose answer **(C)**, give yourself 1 point.

Points earned: _____

If you believe that one picture translates to a thousand words, obtain those pictures (i.e., charts, graphs, illustrations) and bequeath them to your listening audience.

Question 32

Tom recently joined the sales team responsible for promoting automobile rentals. The 10-person team met weekly. At the end-of-the-month meeting one team member would present sales figures and announce top producers and bonus winners. Tom was responsible for making the presentation in May. He asked a coworker for tips on preparing visuals for this meeting. The man replied, "If you're going to bother with visuals, be elaborate! Don't you agree?"

Tom was puzzled by this response. He came up with three possible ways of looking at his coworker's enthusiastic endorsement of elaborate visuals:

(A) If your budget isn't elaborate, you don't have that option.

(B) The KISS (Keep It Simple Strategy) can be powerful.

(C) Presentation time is show time. The more bells and whistles you introduce, the better!

Answers

The strongest answer:

(A) Your budget is composed of dollars, time, and creativity. Dole out a reasonable amount of each and don't behave as though resources are limitless.

The adequate answer:

(B) You're well advised to literally Keep It Simple. Some experts suggest using no more than six lines of text per slide and no more than seven words per line of text.

The weakest answer:

(C) Presentation time is show time. Don't confuse it, however, with the need to pile on the schmaltz. For example, it's easy to get carried away when you have multiple options available via modern presentation software. As a rule, elegant, simple design communicates better than jarring, flashy design.

What Tom Did

Tom decided that as the new guy on the team he needed to dazzle the others with his all-out, no holds barred presentation. At the same time, he needed to spend time wooing rental customers.

He apportioned more time to preparing the visuals for that first presentation than he would spend in the future, paying an outside vendor to prepare colorful charts complete with cartoon characters to represent customer profiles (e.g., heads of household, sole proprietors). The short presentation was a success, but the next time he was in charge of the end-of-the-month meeting, he didn't use visuals. By then he was one of the top producers and his zest for the job was apparent.

Rate yourself: Which one do you favor?

If you chose answer **(A)**, give yourself 5 points.

If you chose answer **(B)**, give yourself 3 points.

If you chose answer **(C)**, give yourself 1 point.

Points earned: _____

Question 33

Karen's company does business around the world, but it is headquartered in a small town in Iowa. Most of the employees at headquarters don't keep abreast of the latest fashion trends. Karen is no exception, but she realizes that when she speaks for the company, her "look" is important.

Karen asks: "How important is my personal appearance when the audience is large (100 or more) and I can't mingle but remain behind the lectern?"

(A) On a scale of 1 to 10, appearance ranks 10 (very important).

(B) I focus heavily on my appearance from the waist up!

(C) A bad hair day isn't acceptable.

Answers

The strongest answer:

(A) Personal appearance is important for several reasons: You usually feel good when you look good, you're likely to mingle with listeners before or after you speak, and you're ready if photographs are taken. After all, you're a *visual* too! There's not one good reason to settle for less than looking your best.

The adequate answer:

(B) This is a sensible approach since all eyes will be on your face. Facial hair grooming (i.e., shave, beard trimming) or application of cosmetics rate extra attention. Choose a blouse, shirt, or suit jacket color that won't clash with background colors on the stage.

The weakest answer:

(C) Perfectly styled hair is desirable but isn't enough to help you look your best.

Rate yourself: Which one do you favor?

If you chose answer (A), give yourself 5 points.

If you chose answer (B), give yourself 4 points.

If you chose answer (C), give yourself 1 point.

Points earned: _____

You may agree that this Chinese proverb is worth noting: "When you have only two pennies left in the world, buy a loaf of bread with one and a lily with the other." It suggests that we prepare presentations with care and give equal time to personal appearance.

Question 34

Where should I stand so I don't obscure visuals from the audience?

(A) If possible, sit down.

(B) Think about the way your audience reads. If it's from left to right, position yourself to the left of the visual. (*Think left* in terms of audience perspective.)

(C) If you suspend yourself from the heavens, so you can't possibly block visuals, it still won't help if the audience must look at poorly planned visuals.

Answers

The strongest answer:

(B) Experts report that this formula is a good rule of thumb.

The adequate answer:

(C) Consider where to position yourself, but more importantly, treat your audience to visuals that deliver at-a-glance comprehension!

The weakest answer:

(A) The question is not where to sit but rather where to stand. It's the only reason this answer ranks as weak.

Rate yourself: Which one do you favor?

If you chose answer **(A)**, give yourself 2 points.

If you chose answer **(B)**, give yourself 5 points.

If you chose answer **(C)**, give yourself 4½ points.

Points earned: _____

In support of the KISS (Keep It Simple Strategy) here's a Winnie the Pooh quote: "A little consideration, a little thought for others, makes all the difference."

Question 35

What are the rules for selecting colors for visual aids?

(A) Assuming you're generating maps, charts, graphs, photos, or illustrations, limit yourself to two to three colors plus black. But don't avoid utilizing items that break this rule if they help round out your presentation.

(B) Type size and style is an important aspect of a visual aid, and color simply makes it look more attractive.

(C) Make sure background and border colors complement your topic. (If you're talking about a winter promotion campaign, you probably shouldn't select pink and green.)

Answers

The strongest answer:

(A) Effective visuals serve the audience. That's the key rule to remember when you assemble your program. Color selection is a major topic, and you can learn all about it in books devoted to the subject.

The adequate answer:

(C) If you're talking about winter but your visuals suggest springtime, something is out of sync. Beware. You'll confuse the audience.

The weakest answer:

(B) Type size and style selection may be admirable, but if the color is off, all suffer!

Rate yourself: Which one do you favor?

If you chose answer (A), give yourself 5 points.

If you chose answer (B), give yourself 1 point.

If you chose answer (C), give yourself 4 points.

Points earned: _____

Colors speak a language of their own. Learn the language and you'll enhance any presentation you give. (Did you know that some people earn their living as color advisers? "Color is serious business." These words are mentioned at www.colorcom.com, a Web site that offers valuable information.) Look for basic information in libraries and bookstores, and check the Internet too.

Question 36

Computer-based presentations (e.g., PowerPoint) are valuable but more costly to produce than flip charts and "old-fashioned" visual aids.

What is an effective way to control costs?

(A) Solicit bids from several audiovisual companies. Don't forget to check on insurance coverage. There could be claims due to damage to laptops, LCD projectors, or other AV equipment. You'll also want to know who is responsible for stolen or lost equipment.

(B) Audiences, accustomed to high-tech presentations, have been known to roll their (collective) eyes when a speaker arrives with an overhead projector and some transparencies. But just because new tools are available doesn't mean you always need to use them. Search for the entertainer within and dazzle audiences with your use of props and nonelectronic aids too.

(C) Company costs can be controlled using methods that apply across the board. Rental costs for LCD projectors, for example, may not provide anticipated ROI (return on investment). How will you know if you're not measuring results? Don't forget to factor in the need for more technical support. But don't toss out the baby with the bathwater. It may take time to assess true value.

Answers

The strongest answer:

(B) When it's time to prepare visuals for a presentation, don't rely solely on what you did before. Ask yourself: "Is that all there is?" And plan accordingly.

The adequate answer:

(C) Measurement is a sensible management approach to confirming ROI. But you may have to reinvent the wheel to settle on a good measurement system to better assess the value and cost of visual aids.

The weakest answer:

(A) This suggestion applies only if you rely upon outside vendors for AV support. Smaller organizations may not deal with vendors. No one would argue, however, that it's prudent to see if insurance protection is in place.

Rate yourself: Which one do you favor?

If you chose answer (A), give yourself 1 point.

If you chose answer (B), give yourself 5 points.

If you chose answer (C), give yourself 3 points.

Points earned: _____

When you oversee a company conference or are part of a team that plans a convention, learn what you can about AV options and costs. A professional meeting planner may provide valuable insight you can use later, when you return to your everyday business environment.

Question 37

Is uppercase writing preferable for visuals?

(A) On a limited basis.

(B) No.

(C) Yes.

Answers

The strongest answer:

> **(B)** Experts claim you should write in upper and lower case. If you use only capitals, words are difficult to read.

The adequate answer:

> **(A)** You may want to selectively use all capitals when preparing visual aids. It can help to set something apart. For example, you may want to display the company name in capitals.

The weakest answer:

> **(C)** See **(B)**! All capitals are not "user-friendly."

Rate yourself: Which one do you favor?

If you chose answer **(A)**, give yourself 3 points.

If you chose answer **(B)**, give yourself 5 points

If you chose answer **(C)**, give yourself zero points.

Points earned: _____

Use what is known. Since words written entirely in capitals are more difficult to read, write using upper and lower case. DO YOU NOTICE THAT EVEN THIS SHORT SENTENCE IS NOT AS EASY ON THE EYES AS THE SENTENCES THAT APPEAR ABOVE USING UPPER AND LOWER CASE LETTERS? SEEING IS BELIEVING!

Question 38

Mary worried about timing. She favored using slide programs but realized that they often distracted her and the audience. She wants to know, "Should I put a visual aid in front of the audience as soon as people enter the room?"

Which of the following suggestions is most important to Mary and other presenters?

(A) Don't show a visual aid until you're ready to use it. When you've finished with it, return to the title slide of your presentation (company logo, or whatever).

(B) Make sure you've got all slides in proper order. It's intrusive to "play" with slides during your presentation. You waste the audience's time and display a lapse in good manners.

(C) Rehearse! Be prepared with a backup plan if your equipment, electricity, or anything else prevents you from showing the slides.

Answers

The strongest answer:

Both **(A)** and **(B)** are favored answers.

(A) If you show a visual aid before you're ready to discuss it, people in the audience may busy themselves with interpreting the visual and not pay attention to what you're saying. The one thing you may want them to focus on is the title of your presentation, or your name, or your company logo. Use a title slide for this purpose and let it linger in view or not, as you choose.

(B) No, this isn't an error. Have you ever been the victim of a presenter who had to readjust slides during a presentation? Upside-down slides, out of order slides, and the like waste your time and distract everyone. It's something a presenter can and must control.

The adequate answer:

(C) You should be familiar with your equipment or have a dependable assistant who will control the visual aids. You and that individual should rehearse. And if you do your act alone, rehearse anyway. While you go about rehearsal, consider what you could do if your visual aid equipment fails. If, for example, you will be showing charts and suddenly the charts aren't accessible, can you skip that portion of your presentation? The best time to assess this is during a rehearsal.

Rate yourself: Which one do you favor?

If you chose answer **(A)**, give yourself 5 points.

If you chose answer **(B)**, give yourself 5 points.

If you chose answer **(C)**, give yourself 3 points.

Points earned: _____

Question 39

One presenter favors a red jacket when he speaks. "It grabs attention," he claims. He is advised not to use the color red in visual aids. "I never understand why," he laments.

Why shouldn't he wear red? Or is it okay?

(A) Use caution when using the color red. That's different from avoiding it.

(B) The color red is an attention grabber. It tends to overpower the eye and may detract from other items in a visual aid so much that it "hurts" the viewer's powers of assessment.

(C) The presenter's choice of a red jacket may not aid him and the message he is trying to deliver. He may want to rethink his habit of opting for this color only.

Answers

The strongest answer:

(B) Just as we don't yell "Fire" in a crowded room, we don't splash the color-of-fire onto our visual aids unless we want to elicit a similar response. This is a good rule of thumb.

The adequate answer:

(A) Yes, use caution when it comes to wearing red. But it can and should be used when it delivers the desired result. Stop signs and stoplights are red with good reason. Don't be so focused on avoiding the color that you neglect to make the most of it when appropriate.

The weakest answer:

(C) On the face of it, this observation has merit. Still, it's probably fair to assume that if the presenter favors a red jacket when he speaks, it's because he speaks on topics that are "compatible" with this shout-about-it color. If, for example, he's a team coach and frequently addresses professional athletes, the color works for him.

Rate yourself: Which one do you favor?

If you chose answer (A), give yourself 4 points.

If you chose answer (B), give yourself 5 points.

If you chose answer (C), give yourself 2 points.

Points earned: _____

Colors affect people on more than one level. For example, red clothing tends to make a person look heavier. You may prefer to wear a splash of red (e.g., a red tie or scarf) and avoid wearing a red jacket or dress.

Question 40

Does the size of the room make a difference when I'm planning what visual aids to use?

> **(A)** Yes. John was told he would be addressing an audience of about 15 people. When he arrived to present, he was told the number had increased to 45 and he would be speaking in a larger room. His flip-chart visuals could not be seen by 45 people. He spoke without them!
>
> **(B)** You may not know that in advance—so be flexible.
>
> **(C)** You can adjust most projectors or electronic devices to your needs, so this is a nonissue.

Answers

The strongest answer:

(A) A lot will depend upon the type of visual aids you're using. In John's case, flip-chart visuals couldn't be readily changed to accommodate the larger crowd. However, he didn't have to avoid using the charts. He could ask his hosts to break the group into two or three groups and speak separately to each group. John should have confirmed the number of attendees as the date for his presentation approached.

The adequate answer:

(C) Plan your visuals for the audience size and room size that accommodates them. Don't assume the room size will cause you to abandon programs you gave in smaller settings. Modern equipment can frequently adjust to new environments. Try out the program in the new location before you permit the audience to be seated.

The weakest answer:

(B) You should know the number of people you will speak to before you appear. It's encouraging when larger numbers wish to attend your presentation, but it's not always a request you should accommodate. You may be less effective when asked to s-t-r-e-t-c-h, and that may disappoint everyone.

Rate yourself: Which one do you favor?

If you chose answer (A), give yourself 5 points.

If you chose answer (B), give yourself 1 point.

If you chose answer (C), give yourself 3 points.

Points earned: _____

Size is not a small matter!

Test Five

Handling Questions and Other Concerns

You may give a flawless presentation, use impeccable visual aids, and follow your carefully prepared note cards, but still not feel relaxed. Why? Perhaps you're dreading the Q&A section to come. You may be asked a question you don't know how to answer.

It's important to plan ahead so you conduct yourself like a champ from beginning to finale! Then again, you may handle a Q&A session with relative ease, but you have other concerns. Your knees shake before the presentation or your voice takes on a monotonous quality. Dozens of little quirks need attention. The good news is that sound advice is available and it's there for the taking.

Question 41

Did you know that some speakers routinely consult with voice coaches? Karen had been jogging for about a year when she started to get frequent compliments about her speaking voice. "You sound so good on the telephone," callers would say.

Her jogging partner, Arlene, was a professional singer. "Does jogging help your voice?" Karen asked her.

"Breathing properly helps," Arlene replied. Keep the shoulders down with the breath intake."

"I hear my voice coach talking to me when we jog!" Karen said, laughing.

What other tips might a vocal coach offer, and which is most important to a speaker?

(A) Open your mouth wider and deliver a stronger vocal tone.

(B) Drink plenty of water, especially the night before your appearance, so you keep your vocal apparatus and yourself hydrated.

(C) Breathe! It's not unusual to forget to breathe regularly when you feel challenged.

Answers

The strongest answer:

(B) Staying hydrated is important for general well-being. (Just think about how some folks sweat before, during, and after they give a speech.) A vocal coach may point out that air-conditioned or heated rooms tend to have low humidity, which is another good reason for a presenter to drink up.

The adequate answer:

(C) Good advice, but even if you don't remember to breathe deeply and rhythmically, you will continue to breathe. (Or you won't appear!)

The weakest answer:

(A) Vocal coaches will make you aware of this fact. Still, it's not the strongest answer because if you follow all the other good advice, this will happen naturally.

Rate yourself: Which one do you favor?

If you chose answer **(A)**, give yourself 2 points.

If you chose answer **(B)**, give yourself 5 points.

If you chose answer **(C)**, give yourself 3 points.

Points earned: _____

Thirty-eight percent of communication is vocal. And according to information on the Web site www.presentationhelper.co.uk/voice-coaching-tips.htm, a voice can sound too aggressive, unconvincing, bored, emotional, and monotonous. Clearly, you don't have to be touring with an opera company to benefit from professional coaching services. You may want to record and listen to yourself. If you think you could sound better, engage a professional for an evaluation. Afterward, decide what next.

Question 42

"What should I do if I ask whether anyone has questions and no one does?" This possibility dogged Rebecca until her coworker Deborah said, "Becky, I'll ask a question if no one else does." From then on she realized it was feasible to "plant" someone in the audience to work with her.

What else can Rebecca do to get people involved in this part of the program?

(A) Ask a question. Start by saying, "People often ask me . . ." Select a hot topic and address it. Pause. Make eye contact with members of the audience and ask if anyone has a question.

(B) Ask the audience a question that can't be answered with a simple yes or no.

(C) Make your closing statement and leave.

Answers

The strongest answer:

(A) This ploy serves as an icebreaker, especially when you're speaking to a less sophisticated group that suffers from the "I don't want to be the first to speak out" syndrome.

The adequate answer:

(B) Asking funnel questions (i.e., wide-open at the top) stimulates participation. For example, "How does the new XYZ software program compare with the ABC software?"

The weakest answer:

(C) It's true that a closing statement comes after a Q&A session, but it's useful to encourage audience participation. It provides a learning opportunity for all concerned.

Rate yourself: Which one do you favor?

If you chose answer (A), give yourself 5 points.

If you chose answer (B), give yourself 4 points.

If you chose answer (C), give yourself 2 points.

Points earned: _____

If you conclude the program at the end of a Q&A session, you miss an excellent opportunity to give your audience something to remember you by. Leave them with a closing statement. And if you already delivered one before asking for questions, repeat it. You may want to say the same thing using a slightly different vocabulary.

Question 43

What should I do with my hands? Even the most seasoned speakers are occasionally stymied by these appendages that may all of a sudden take on a life of their own.

(A) Forget about them. Happily, not everyone is self-conscious about where to place their hands. If others can "fuhgetaboutit," you may be able to do the same. Concentrate on what you're saying and how you're saying it.

(B) Use them to "naturally" punctuate your comments, or just let your arms rest comfortably at your sides.

(C) Don't wave your arms around or use them to distract the audience.

Answers

The strongest answer:

(B) You don't want your hands to be the focal point for the audience, but they can be a natural asset if you can relax and use them as you do when speaking to a friend. (This presumes you don't have regrettable habits like repeatedly pointing your finger at your friend's face or chest, etc.)

The adequate answer:

(A) If you're not self-conscious about where to place your hands, you're fortunate. You have one less thing to perfect as you work to become an excellent presenter.

The weakest answer:

(C) Although this is a valid observation, it merely tells what not to do.

Rate yourself: Which one do you favor?

If you chose answer (A), give yourself 3 points.

If you chose answer (B), give yourself 5 points.

If you chose answer (C), give yourself 1 point.

Points earned: _____

Your hands speak a language of their own and may tell listeners you're anxious or relaxed. Some speakers solve the problem by holding onto something like the gizmo that controls a slide program. Watch what other presenters do with their hands and mimic the best models. Eventually you'll find a style that suits you.

Question 44

Should I rely on a timekeeper so I can stay within my allotted time to speak?

- **(A)** You should prepare your remarks so they fit into a particular time parameter.

- **(B)** If you ask someone to keep an eye on the clock for you, tell him or her to alert you when five minutes remain.

- **(C)** You may have to serve as your own timekeeper. One experienced trainer valued her watch collection. She owned six timepieces that had various features (e.g., easy to read numerals) she could depend upon for help when she had to be her own timekeeper.

Answers

The strongest answer:

(A) It's important to fit your presentation to your time allotment. If you don't, you'll probably have to rush at the end and risk leaving out important information. So even if you ask someone in the audience to signal you when you reach the midpoint or some other point, plan ahead.

The adequate answer:

(B) Asking for a five-minute alert is a good idea, provided you have also planned the entire program with care. See answer (A). Don't dilly-dally. Begin your close.

The weakest answer:

(C) You could serve as your own timekeeper, but why not obtain help? This will free you to focus on your remarks and audience response.

Rate yourself: Which one do you favor?

If you chose answer (A), give yourself 5 points.

If you chose answer (B), give yourself 4 points.

If you chose answer (C), give yourself 2 points.

Points earned: _____

Synchronize watches! Make sure all concerned parties have the same information.

Question 45

Susan was told that she's a perfectionist and spends too much time worrying. She agreed that worry was a waste of time but said she liked being considered a perfectionist. She began to maintain copious notes and lists. Here are some items that appear on her "Preparing to Lead a Seminar List." (Do you agree with Susan?)

Which of these should be the major concern presenters think about?

(A) I'm speaking to a captive audience and should have regard for their time.

(B) Apologies are an unacceptable way to begin—for example, "Sorry I'm late."

(C) This is a live interaction, so I'm free to ad-lib.

Answers

The strongest answer:

(A) If 25 people attend your one-hour presentation, a total of 25 hours are devoted to you and what you have to say. Add to this hours spent traveling to and fro (even if it's just time spent in an elevator) and you can see that you command considerable time from you listeners. (If each attendee earns $25 an hour, the dollar cost of time away from work is more than $625.) A presenter would be crass to ignore the value of attendees' time.

The adequate answer:

(B) Apologies for being late, distributing workbooks that have missing pages, or anything that wastes a person's time is unacceptable. Of course, power failures and circumstances beyond your control will be excused.

The weakest answer:

(C) It's practically impossible not to ad-lib during a live presentation. This is not a substitute, however, for being prepared. Don't rely upon your charming personality to carry you through an entire program. If you do, you'll probably waste too much of your listeners' time.

Rate yourself: Which one do you favor?

If you chose answer (A), give yourself 5 points.

If you chose answer (B), give yourself 4 points.

If you chose answer (C), give yourself 1 point.

Points earned: _____

People are inclined to say, "The devil is in the details." If you're already a comfortable presenter, examine and perhaps tweak the details. Otherwise concentrate on main points but don't overlook the details.

Question 46

What happens when the question is clear but you don't know the answer? This happened to Alan early in his career as a motivational speaker and he never forgot the sinking feeling in his stomach. He quickly adopted a strategy to use if confronted with this situation again.

Which strategy do you think he settled on?

(A) I dismiss it and move on. There's little point in making a big display of what I don't know. It doesn't help me or the listener.

(B) I don't try to answer. I tell the attendee that I'll do my best to get it and will contact him or her when I do.

(C) I ask attendees if anyone can answer the question. I preface this by saying that someone in the audience may know more about this particular question or matter than I do.

Answers

The strongest answer:

(B) Own up! No one knows everything. If you promise to follow up, make sure you know how to contact the attendee who asked the question.

The adequate answer:

(C) This approach is reasonable. The only glitch may come about if the answers you receive from attendees are inaccurate. Ask the person who provides answers, "How do you know this?" Be sure to thank that individual for his or her assistance.

The weakest answer:

(A) It's rude to ignore bona fide questions. It may be, however, that some audience participants deliver a steady flow of them and slow you down. In that case, move on.

Rate yourself: Which one do you favor?

If you chose answer (A), give yourself 2 points.
If you chose answer (B), give yourself 5 points.
If you chose answer (C), give yourself 4 points.

Points earned: _____

Find out the answer to the question and consider it a learning opportunity. The next time the question is posed, you'll have the answer.

Question 47

Should speakers move around on stage or in the audience?

(A) There's no one-size-fits-all answer. Moving about must be comfortable for the speaker, and the audience must be able to see and hear what's going on. Well-orchestrated activity can lift the energy level in the room.

(B) Moving about is impractical since you can't read your notes or make eye contact with the audience.

(C) Moving about may be necessary. If, for example, the presenter must demonstrate how to use new equipment, he or she can't stand still.

Answers

The strongest answer:

(A) Strolling up and down the aisles or moving around on stage may help the speaker release nervous energy and appear calmer to onlookers. The action literally keeps heads turning too. Being glued to one place is tiring for speaker and listeners.

The adequate answer:

(C) If you're moving about, don't permit yourself to do the no-no's such as keeping your back to the audience or standing in front of the visual aids images so you serve as a screen. (This has happened to speakers who should know better!)

The weakest answer:

(B) Eye contact with members of the audience is possible whether a speaker is roller-skating or remaining still on stage. As to reading notes, you can stroll to a central spot (e.g., the lectern) and glance at them periodically. A glance should be sufficient.

Rate yourself: Which one do you favor?

If you chose answer (A), give yourself 5 points.

If you chose answer (B), give yourself 2 points.

If you chose answer (C), give yourself 4 points.

Points earned: _____

Good vibrations! It's that special something a speaker "feels" when the audience is caught up in the program. National figure Elizabeth Dole must have experienced good vibrations when she mingled with the crowds with whom she spoke during a televised political convention. Try it (walking up and down aisles and lingering here and there), maybe you'll like it.

Question 48

Nick believed passionately in his topic—help for those who cannot help themselves—and so even when his presentation was a little wordy or he neglected to answer questions effectively, audiences were moved by his presentations. Volunteers came forward and donations increased.

Will passion, alone, see you through?

(A) It's more important that your presentation is well-organized and to deliver it effectively than to "wear your heart on your sleeve."

(B) If you try too hard to show your passion, you may look like a phony. Don't purposely stifle emotions, but do keep them in check.

(C) People need to believe you, and when you know your subject well and speak with enthusiasm, you're going to turn in a winning performance. Passion isn't everything, but it is the most important thing.

Answers

The strongest answer:

(C) When you're genuinely passionate about your topic and convey that to listeners, you will usually be forgiven small infractions. There's nothing quite as contagious as enthusiasm.

The adequate answer:

(B) True passion is difficult to disguise. At the same time, do everything possible to prepare your speech to be the best it can be.

The weakest answer:

(A) Don't detract from the importance of being earnest! Most of this response is fair and reasonable, but the moment you give passion a low priority you work against yourself.

Rate yourself: Which one do you favor?

If you chose answer (A), give yourself ½ point.

If you chose answer (B), give yourself 4 points.

If you chose answer (C), give yourself 5 points.

Points earned: _____

Passion goes well with another P word: practice. Take every opportunity available to speak to groups. Practice makes perfect (or close to it). And when you're passionate about your topic, you want to share it with the world.

Question 49

According to Maggie Eyre, author of *Speak Easy: The Essential Guide to Speaking in Public*, 60 percent of learning takes place through visuals.

Barry realizes the importance of using visual aids when he presents but has never been comfortable with them. What should he do?

(A) Get help. An assistant can operate PowerPoint for him and even help him prepare slides.

(B) Learn by taking classes or hiring an instructor.

(C) If Barry feels his presentations are successful without visual aids, he shouldn't feel bound to incorporate them into his programs.

Answers

The strongest answer:

(B) Learning is a life-long pursuit. Even if Barry opts to have an assistant work with him on visual aids, it's beneficial for him to know more about common visual aids programs like PowerPoint. Menu-driven "teaching" programs are readily available, and more traditional seminars and workshops are offered too. In addition to building self-confidence, Barry may discover new tools to enhance his presentations.

The adequate answer:

(A) It's acceptable to have an assistant work with you to achieve goals. Rehearse sufficiently so the time spent together in front of the audience is seamless.

The weakest answer:

(C) No need to reinvent the wheel. If the emphasis is on visual aids as a great learning tool, it's a mistake to ignore it.

Rate yourself: Which one do you favor?

If you chose answer (A), give yourself 4 points.

If you chose answer (B), give yourself 5 points.

If you chose answer (C), give yourself 1 point.

Points earned: _____

Nothing stays the same. Be aware of anything new that can help you improve your presentations. At the same time, don't be too quick to change what works. If it ain't broke, don't fix it!

Question 50

Arlene was getting married and asked her uncle Sid to deliver the wedding speech. "Relax and enjoy yourself," she told him. "You say the nicest things, and if you do this for us, I'm sure it will be memorable."

Sid had some speaking experience, but he didn't think a wedding speech should be approached in the same way as a presentation for business purposes. Do you agree?

(A) Sid should use everything he knows about speaking well as he prepares to deliver the wedding speech.

(B) He will be in friendly territory at a wedding. At the same time, Arlene and her new husband are counting on him to do a good job, and that may put some extra pressure on Sid. In some ways this "personal emphasis" makes the speech different.

(C) Sid should feel flattered to be asked and do the best he can to make the newlyweds happy. He may want to ask friends who are close to the bride and groom for input: "What could I say that would be important to Arlene and her groom?"

Answers

The strongest answer:

(A) A speech by any other name is still a speech. A wedding speech deserves the same careful preparation as any other presentation.

The adequate answer:

(C) Asking others for input is okay but Sid was probably asked to make this speech because the bride believed he already knew what to say. Consider, first, what you should say so you won't be completely swayed by the opinions of others.

The weakest answer:

(B) This kind of thinking puts the spotlight off center and is unproductive. The focus should be on the assignment (i.e., preparation of the speech) and not on feeling extra pressure.

Rate yourself: Which one do you favor?

If you chose answer (A), give yourself 5 points.

If you chose answer (B), give yourself zero points.

If you chose answer (C), give yourself 4 points.

Points earned: _____

It's an honor to be asked to deliver a wedding speech or other personal occasion type speech. Sometimes when an audience is made up of people the speaker knows well, he or she speaks too rapidly. Don't! Savor the moments.

Presentation IQ Scorecard

Question 1: _____   Question 20: _____   Question 39: _____

Question 2: _____   Question 21: _____   Question 40: _____

Question 3: _____   Question 22: _____   Question 41: _____

Question 4: _____   Question 23: _____   Question 42: _____

Question 5: _____   Question 24: _____   Question 43: _____

Question 6: _____   Question 25: _____   Question 44: _____

Question 7: _____   Question 26: _____   Question 45: _____

Question 8: _____   Question 27: _____   Question 46: _____

Question 9: _____   Question 28: _____   Question 47: _____

Question 10: _____   Question 29: _____   Question 48: _____

Question 11: _____   Question 30: _____   Question 49: _____

Question 12: _____   Question 31: _____   Question 50: _____

Question 13: _____   Question 32: _____   Total Score: _____

Question 14: _____   Question 33: _____

Question 15: _____   Question 34: _____

Question 16: _____   Question 35: _____

Question 17: _____   Question 36: _____

Question 18: _____   Question 37: _____

Question 19: _____   Question 38: _____

Tally Your Presentation IQ Score

Throughout this book you selected answers to questions and had the opportunity to record a score.

- All the individual scores can now be inserted on the preceding page. (You have permission to copy this page and insert numbers on the copy if you prefer not to write in the book.)

- Add all scores together to obtain a final score.

- Compare your score to the key that is designed to interpret the score. It's the ultimate feedback!

Test One Scores   = (Perfect Score = 50)
Test Two Scores   = (Perfect Score = 50)
Test Three Scores = (Perfect Score = 50)
Test Four Scores   = (Perfect Score = 50)
Test Five Scores   = (Perfect Score = 50)
Grand Total   = (Perfect Score = 250)

Key and Score Interpretation

- If your Grand Total is 200 or more, congratulations! You have an excellent grasp of what it takes to be a successful presenter. Keep up the good work and continue to improve performance by adapting tips and strategies provided to you in this book.

  You may want to begin by reviewing chapters in which your score was far lower than the Perfect Score. For example, the Perfect Score for Chapter Three is 50. If your score is 25 or thereabouts, take time to review beginnings, middles, and ends.

- If your Grand Total is between 50 and 200, you have the basic knowledge; now you just need to hone your skills. Read Part 2 and then retake the test. Concentrate on the topics in this book in which your scores were lowest, but don't stop there. Review everything mentioned in the book and consider joining a speakers' organization (e.g., Toastmaster's International), a community theater group, a choir, or other participatory group that makes it possible for you to work on communication skills. Once these efforts are under way, challenge yourself to attract speaking engagements. You may want to speak in front of groups on a regular basis (e.g., six times a year). Before long you'll be wowing your audiences every time.

- If your Grand Total is below 50, it signifies that you are a novice presenter. No one is born a natural presenter so it's okay to be at a beginner level. Preparation and practice are all you need to master presentation skills. Read Part 2 and retake the test until you achieve a higher score. You may also want to consider taking a presentation class to learn some basic presentation skills. These are offered at many universities and even on the Internet. A class also gives you a great opportunity to get practice speaking in front of a sympathetic audience.

PART 2

Proven Techniques for Boosting Your Presentation IQ

Chapter One

Quick Keys to Successful Presentations

Many jobs require that people give presentations at one point or another. Because so many must put something together with little preparation time, we focus on seven Quick Keys to a successful presentation in this chapter:

1. It's about time.

2. It's about the audience.

3. It's about your topic.

4. It's about you too.

5. It's about the words.

6. It's about a logical flow.

7. Less is best.

You Are Here

You've just been invited to make a presentation. Use this blueprint to get to your designation. It begins with the first of the seven Quick Keys:

It's about Time

- How much time do you have to prepare for the appearance?

- How much time will you spend addressing the audience?

Whether you'll be talking to an audience of thousands or a small group, you must know the answers to these questions from the get-go. Clearly, if you have one week to prepare, your options expand. Conversely, options shrink if you have only one day to prepare. Do you have time to assemble impressive visual aids? Do you have time to tailor your wardrobe and grooming for the appearance? The answers to these questions and lots more depend upon the time factor.

Did you ever hear someone deliver an excellent presentation even though it was impromptu and spontaneous? Chances are you heard that person's "Elevator Speech." It's a speech the individual can give in the time it takes to move up or down 12 (plus or minus) floors in an elevator. The speaker is no stranger to this speech. Virtually all seasoned speakers can deliver an Elevator Speech without blinking an eye.

You can do it too. Take the topic you speak on most often and tweak it to appeal to another audience. For example, if you typically speak about the importance of listening to the customer and you make this presentation to salespeople, speak to nonsalespeople about the importance of listening to others to achieve their goals. Be brief and to the point. Be ready to deliver it in your winning style whenever asked. Voilà, instant speech and admiration from those who know you took on the speaking assignment without hesitation or delay.

It's about the Audience

- What do you know about the people who will be listening to you?

- Do you know them personally? (Are they coworkers or members of your professional association?)

- What do they have in common with one another? If nothing else, it's probably safe to assume they're all interested in your topic.

- Insofar as experience is concerned, are they beginners or advanced? (For example, are they student teachers versus 20-year veteran teachers? To make a quick assessment, ask variations of this question by using appropriate words: experienced versus inexperienced, amateurs versus professionals, mature versus younger.)

Frequently, the person who invites you to make a presentation can supply you with *Audience Profile* data. How can you move ahead to prepare anything (e.g., remarks, visual aids) until you *Know your audience*? Even if you're about to present a "canned speech"—one you've given many times before—you won't be able to make necessary adjustments until you develop an Audience Profile.

> You frequently must settle for less than the usual amount of information when asked to speak to a group on short notice. In this situation, the following shortcut is effective: ascertain the theme of the program.
>
> A luggage salesman, who usually speaks to department store buyers, can discuss the benefit of using his company's luggage when addressing a group of people that is attending a talk titled, "Preparing for Your Trip Abroad." He'll omit bulk sales pricing information but mention why his product is superior to competitors' luggage and what benefits each traveler will enjoy when using it. If the members of this audience have little else in common, they're probably all getting ready to take a trip.

It's about Your Topic

- Will attendees care?

- Why? What's in it for them?

Most presenters feel some passion for their topic, and that's a good thing. But it's necessary to hone in on some facet of the topic that will do something for the members of the audience, such as entertain, instruct, or motivate. Force yourself to be specific when you answer the question: What do you want to tell them? You'll know you're on the right track when you feel sure they will care. Think in terms of benefits: How do listeners benefit? Tell them! If possible, rename your presentation to appeal to your current audience. Our luggage salesman could talk about:

- Luggage that serves you for a lifetime of travel.

- Luggage you'll be proud to sell to your discriminating customers.

- Luggage designed by artists for artists who travel.

The first audience is made up of travelers. The next audience is made up of salespeople. And the last audience is made up of designers and artists—

an elite group of travelers. The speaker will deliver the same information to each group but will spotlight different benefits for each group.

It's about You Too

What does the audience know about you? Promotional material touting your presentation should feature your expertise, but in situations when you speak on short notice, information about your background may be omitted.

Madge was the manager of a well-known dry cleaning operation. When she spoke to an audience of fashion designers, they had every reason to believe she knew about dry cleaning. She spoke about different fabrics and how each responded to repeated cleaning. She discussed fabric trimmings and adornments and noted how some fared better than others in the cleaning process. Still, when she mentioned that she had an associate's degree in textile chemistry, her stature with this group was elevated quickly.

> Let people know what you can do, and they may come to you to do it for them. Another way of expressing this is: Attract customers, clients, and other interested parties to do business with you by "educating" them when you present. Let them know you're an expert and give them data to prove it!

Moving Right Along

Ever notice that when you're at the zoo or a shopping mall or some other large place, there are numerous maps or directories are posted to tell you where you are? If you look at the map when you're near the northern end of the site, for example, you'll see YOU ARE HERE. When you stroll to the eastern end, you'll see another map with the YOU ARE HERE marking that location. The site doesn't change, but your location does. If you're satisfied with the importance of the first four Quick Keys, you're ready to change your location. To reiterate those keys:

- It's about time.

- It's about the audience.

- It's about your topic.

- It's about you too.

Get a grip on these before you change your location, and move forward, to the next Quick Key.

It's about the Words

To some extent, all of the above has been discussed at length earlier, and a gentle reminder is all that is required. The following tips, suggestions, and observations about the words you use, however, require your full and dedicated attention now!

Say What You Mean

Clear (unambiguous) communication from start to finish is laudatory. You may not be in charge of generating presentation announcements, but if they are descriptive and complete so that the audience arrives with clear expectations, you're off to an excellent start.

Mesh the Presentation with Expectations

Check your speech notes and handout copy to be sure they mesh with the title of the presentation and the advance publicity.

Sam's speech was titled, "Everything You Want to Know About Working from the Company's London Offices." When he checked his notes, however, he noticed that he never mentioned the London offices. He was planning to talk about how the typical workweek in London differs from the workweek in the United States and to make a host of other observations about working in London. When he realized the omission, he added specific information about the company's parklike campus location, the tea room on the premises that enjoys a five-star rating, and the distance you must walk to reach the train station.

Paint Pictures

Stories enable you to involve listeners and leave them with something to remember. Mention that, when you entered the plant, the new production machinery was so silent you actually stepped outside to see if you were at the correct address. Attendees will virtually step outside with you and aren't likely to forget that the machinery isn't noisy anymore.

Say What's Necessary

Avoid useless embellishment. You may be tempted to say more about the plant, but if the point of your talk is to extol the virtues of the new production machinery—don't stray.

Ever see an audience with eyes glazed over? You've lost 'em!

The above Quick Keys may be the ones that single-handedly put a stop to this. Tell members of your audience what they came to hear (even if your speech shakes up the status quo), and paint pictures so they can hardly wait to see where it all leads.

Words Win Favor
Experts report that, when surveyed, people admit they respond more favorably to some words (e.g., *new, improved, natural, pure*). If you're addressing consumers, such words should work well in your presentation. Once you establish an Audience Profile, look for words the audience will embrace. Search the Internet or contact appropriate professional associations for information. At the least, scan industry-specific articles and highlight words that are repeated and that appeal to you.

Maintain Word Lists
The curious thing about maintaining a word list is that it starts you thinking about specific words and their value. This isn't a frivolous pursuit, because even if you're not making a formal presentation often, you're probably writing reports or sending e-mail, and these efforts will benefit from careful word choices too.

All Together Now

How do you relate to your listeners? Pronouns tell the tale: Are *we* in this together? Or do *I* want *you* to do this for *me*? Who is better—*we* or *they*? *You* had better comply or *your* holiday party will be cancelled.

Inclusiveness

If it's your intention to be thought of as one of the group, use words that say so. You automatically separate yourself from others when you repeatedly use words that act like a line of demarcation. If group harmony and accord is what you seek, pay attention to how pronoun selection can support or undermine you.

Hank spoke to 15 hikers about to embark on an ambitious Grand Canyon trek. "Each of us must carry sufficient water," he stressed.

"We will move along as a group. The slowest among us sets the pace. Keep this in mind when you make your decision as to whether your physical condition enables you to participate. Remember, the rest of us depend on you to move at a brisk pace." Then he added, "There are at least two people here now who shouldn't go on this hike." A hush came over the group. "I won't make that decision for them. But I have never been wrong about observations of this type."

Eventually, 13 hikers set out together, and the trip was a success. Hank kept people a little off balance by using "pronoun psychology": *We* hike as a group. *You* are responsible for keeping up. *I* know what I'm talking about. (Each listener had to work to decide where he or she fit and couldn't make that determination until Hank finished speaking.) Since 13 out of 15 people went on the hike, and since the trip was successful, we may conclude that Hank's presentation achieved the desired result.

You Can Get There from Here

If you could check a map or directory, you'd notice we're about to move to the sixth priority point location; our sixth Quick Key. We'll quickly follow with the final key. Since our hiking leader Hank, above, also helps demonstrate the sixth point, we won't have to move too far.

It's about a Logical Flow

Let logic lead the way. In the previous example, notice how Hank built his presentation from the ground up. He let people know specifically what was expected of them and then told them that not everyone was in shape for the hike. If he hadn't discussed expectations first (carry water, walk at a brisk pace), listeners may not have agreed with him. Jot down the points you want to make.

One way to see if a logical—or orderly—flow is maintained is to juxtapose statements. Sarah told her coworkers:

1. No "Casual Friday" attire will be tolerated during the month of May.

2. The CEO will work from our location during May and June.

3. College graduates will visit with her during the month of May.

4. Your cooperation is essential since it helps maintain our prized company image.

What happens when Sarah changes the order of statements to two, three, one, and four? Even though each statement is accurate as a stand-alone, when presented in this order, employees will know why Casual Friday dress is cancelled during the month of May. Sarah should not mention June. Her goal is to make sure employees don't dress casually on Fridays in May. Extra information, even when it's accurate, can muddy logical flow.

It's about Less Is Best

Sarah's story also helps demonstrate that less is best, another Quick Key that presenters should embrace. It encompasses many aspects of making presentations. In the following explanation it's used to examine accessories.

Michael purchased a projector to take with him when he spoke on behalf of the Chamber of Commerce. He considered the basics: fan noise, brightness (preferably 2,000 lumens), lamp life (these lamps can be costly to replace), and ease of transportation. The weight was a factor as well as the style configuration (e.g., sleek and small). Since his laptop screen is XGA, he needs an XGA projector to match. He chose the projector that met his needs and didn't exceed them.

You can see how this applies to your presentation length too. Don't go over the allotted time. That's a sure sign of an amateur, and it's also a flagrant display of bad manners.

> It's easier to write and/or speak at length than it is to write or say something short or to say less. The great American writer Mark Twain is reported to have expressed it this way: "Forgive my long letter; I did not have time to write a short one."

20 Strategies for Combating Stage Fright

The following are listed in no particular order of importance. Remember, not all speakers have the same concerns. Adapt those that appeal to you. If they work well for you, keep them!

1. If you can't eliminate caffeine-laden beverages, keep them to a minimum.

2. If possible, ask to speak first. For obvious reasons, your jitters will be short-lived.

3. Arrive early. Examine the stage, lighting, and seating arrangements. Check your props (e.g., microphone, visual aids apparatus). Take comfort in knowing that everything is in good working order and things are ready for you.

4. Others don't know you're nervous unless you tell them. Resist the urge to fess up!

5. Inhale deeply and hold it—one, two, and three—exhale slowly! It's an old remedy for attaining a deeper level of inner peace and calm.

6. Practice, practice, practice. What's the worst thing that can happen? Whatever it is can't be that bad. You've got your topic and your presentation *nailed*.

7. Take advantage of as many speaking opportunities as possible. After a while you'll realize you were jittery before and did well. You can do it again . . . and again . . . and . . .

8. Mingle with members of the audience in advance of your presentation. Ask not what you can do for yourself (e.g., relax); ask what you can do for them. Focus on them.

9. Find your passion. When you speak on matters that excite you, your natural enthusiasm takes over, and there's practically no room left for nervousness—if it does show up.

10. Understand the phenomenon. You're nervous because you contemplate "imagined threats": "I'll forget my words, people will see my knees shake." Accentuate the positive and banish "imagined threats" from your thoughts.

11. Get help. Work with a speech coach or other professional if your fear of speaking gets the best of you. Refuse to surrender to it.

12. Get plenty of sleep and drink plenty of water. When you do, you're investing in your physical well-being, and that's always an important strategy.

13. Take a hike! If you normally jog or go to the gym but you're away from home, plug in some other form of exercise rather than just doing without any.

14. Just say no. If you're especially anxious, it may be tempting to take a sedative, but that's ill-advised unless your medical expert says otherwise. Not only will you be using a crutch that could make you "foggy"—you'll do nothing to build confidence in your own powers to overcome fears, and you may give rise to a bad habit.

15. Make funny faces. No, not at the audience. In private before the presentation. Make funny faces, stick out your tongue, open your eyes wide and then shut them tight. In short, exercise your tense body parts, and they should start to relax.

16. Visualize being introduced to the audience. Hear the applause. Begin your presentation. Show your visual aids. Continue your presentation. Ask for questions. Answer them. Deliver your closing statement. See the audience rise to its feet as it applauds, and see you take a bow. In short, take a mind tour and come out successful on the other end. You are mentally primed for success and should be able to relax and just do it!

17. Prepare for sweaty palms by keeping a handkerchief within easy reach. Don't use paper (e.g., dinner napkin, facial tissue) substitutes since they usually aren't as absorbent or . . . quiet.

18. Forewarned is forearmed. Is there a chance you'll have hecklers in your audience? If so, you may want to be sure a sergeant at arms is available. Then, in the unlikely event you're heckled and can't handle the individual gracefully on your own, help is waiting in the wings to deal with the situation.

19. Talk to a trusted pal before you appear. A spouse, sister, brother, or friend may serve as your personal booster. Chat with that person the night before or hours before you'll speak. Cheery words and approval can add immeasurably to your feeling of well-being. When you feel good, you can do anything!

20. Remind yourself that once you begin to speak, a lovely calm is likely to descend upon you. Console yourself with the knowledge that stage fright symptoms are not going to hang around too long. It may help to actually do a countdown. "Five minutes before I step onto the stage, four, three, two, go . . . "

Many seasoned entertainers report that the jitters they get before appearing in front of an audience help them get ready to be successful. If you can adopt this way of thinking, you'll recognize that some nervousness simply comes with the territory and you're in good company.

20 Strategies for "Speaking" Body Language

1. Smiles are understood in virtually every language. Be generous with smiles.

2. Frowns and grimaces signal a negative response. Avoid frowns and grimaces unless you're purposely making use of them. A dramatic frown to emphasize a statement or action may elicit laughter from your listeners. Take care not to be clownlike unless that's your intention.

3. Hand-wringing translates to being ill at ease. Avoid hand-wringing and you'll be in a good position to fake it until you make it. Remember, onlookers don't know you're nervous until you wring your hands to tell them so.

4. Avoiding eye contact is considered rude (and renders you a suspicious character). Make eye contact! Still, there are extenuating circumstances. In some cultures it's considered a sign of disrespect to make eye contact with the elders. And if a speaker is vision-challenged (e.g., blind), he or she won't utilize this strategy for demonstrating interest in the listening audience.

5. Use a firm grip when you shake hands and you'll exude self-confidence. It's customary to shake hands with the individual who introduces you to an audience. Extend your hand as you approach the master or mistress of ceremonies. The audience will notice your quick step and firm handshake. These help make a good first impression.

6. Hands can tell people you're absentminded. If you fuss with your clothing, repeatedly stroke your hair or brow, tap your fingers on the desk, or fidget with this and that, onlookers will be distracted by this unproductive (and usually distracting) activity. *Make plans for hanz!*

7. Deep, exaggerated breathing (e.g., huff and puff) suggests anger or distress. Take steps to minimize your distress without permitting telltale deep breathing to give you away.

8. Shaking a fist suggests that you're angry. If you're in front of an audience and don't want people to guess that you're angry, take care not to shake, or to pound your fist on a hard surface.

9. Respect personal space. If you're sharing the microphone with another presenter, step away and give that individual space. When you speak to the group, ideally your colleague will do the same for you. Most people don't like to feel crowded. A good rule of thumb is: arm's length away. But the rule may not apply in your circles.

10. Pauses: Do they qualify as body language? Technically pause signify—nothing. But "dead air" or silence surrounded by conversation sends a nonverbal message (i.e., the definition of body language). If you pause too much, you may be perceived to be forgetful or worse (e.g., uninformed). Don't race through presentations, but don't pause too long or too often.

11. Sitting stiffly at the edge of your chair makes you appear uncomfortable. Sit like this while waiting to be called to the microphone, and the members of the audience will probably instinctively pull away from you. After all, you're here with them, and they feel responsible for your discomfort.

12. Hands crossed in front of your chest can indicate: stand back, stay away, don't get too close. If you notice this body language from audience members, you've got your work cut out for you. Barriers must come down before you can be effective. As a speaker, you don't want to set up barriers. Unfold those arms!

13. Shuffle your feet, slouch your shoulders, or slump in your chair and you might as well shout to the world at large that you're not a robust individual. If you want to exude well-being, walk with a spring in your step, hold your shoulders back, and sit up straight in your chair.

14. Pacing the floor can indicate you're feeling like a caged animal (i.e., ill at ease). When you're trying to get rid of excess energy before your presentation, you may not want to pace within sight of the people who will soon be in your audience.

15. The clothes you wear and how you groom yourself send messages. Others may not refer to these factors as "body language," but they qualify. Choose your clothing with care. If you show up looking as though you're going to clean your garage and the attendees are dressed for a formal affair, you're probably in trouble. Unless you dressed that way to prove a point you're making during your presentation, you effectively tell people you don't respect them and have little regard for the circumstances.

16. A few words about touch: If you slap people on the back, grab shoulders, and hold onto arms, you make a spectacle of yourself. This kind of behavior may be acceptable at a family gathering (e.g., for the father of the bride), but it's not acceptable in a business setting. Show enthusiasm with your voice as opposed to your touch.

17. Strange as it may seem, your voice can introduce "body language" to a scenario. Grunts, groans, whistles, *tsk-tsk* noises, and clicking

sounds distract people and punctuate the air with irritants. The person making these noises contorts his or her face to produce these sounds. It's not a pretty picture. Don't let unwelcome sounds emanate from you.

18. Rise to greet someone who approaches you. Hold a door open for the person walking behind you. These polite actions enable you to display favorable body language.

19. When engaged in conversation with a person, don't abruptly turn your head away to give your attention to another person or thing. If you must interrupt, do so with a request: "Would you please excuse me for a moment?"

20. Clap your hands and demonstrate you're pleased. Applause from the audience tells you that you're doing okay. But applause can indicate something is amiss. If a heckler rises to refute something you say and members of the audience applaud, these people are speaking to you with their body language. Are they trying to drown out the heckler or are they showing they agree? It's up to you to quickly interpret the message and act accordingly.

Bonus tip: Close your eyes and hold your head and others deduce that you don't feel well or that you're lost in thought. This is a good reminder that "body language" can have more than one meaning and you should avoid making snap judgments. Put the spoken word together with complementary gestures or body language, and you'll boost your communication powers exponentially.

No doubt you can add to this list of gestures and nonverbal communication that speaks loudly and clearly to all. To make a serious study of body language, especially as "spoken" in the world of business, read some of the dozens of good books on the topic. Don't be surprised to find some excellent information in books spotlighting negotiation skills and how to play card games like poker.

Chapter Two

Preparation

Even if you only have a few minutes to prepare, it's possible to be ready for your presentation. This chapter gives tips on quick preparation strategies. In addition, it provides sidebars crammed with instructions for delivering a winning performance, including speaking loudly, clearly, and slowly, and interacting with your audience. A Last Minute Checklist is included to make sure you have everything from your notes to your visuals to directions to the conference.

Turn to this chapter when you need a Cheat Sheet! Here you'll find support at a glance. It can't substitute for the more in-depth information you find throughout the book, but it can get you up and out the door feeling more confident when you've got to show up and perform on short notice.

Are you a golfer?
Do you practice yoga?
Are you proficient in karate?
Do you enjoy playing bridge, poker, or other card games?

These pursuits, and more, give you concentration experience. You can feel buoyed knowing the mental discipline you've already developed in other areas will come in handy right now.

Getting Ready

Put your powers of concentration and your "focus muscles" to work as
you get ready to make a presentation. Expel distractions and concentrate.
Answer the following 15 questions. (They come complete with practical
instructions!)

1. Do you have an Audience Profile? (Anything you discover can be
   helpful, including occupation, group affiliation, ages, interests, and
   attitudes—conservative, liberal.)

> Your contact person may be able to fax a membership roster to you.
> It will be of interest if it lists members' job titles or how long people
> have been members. Rosters of this type are frequently maintained
> by professional organizations' staff and may be considered propri-
> etary information. Explain your interest (e.g., "I want to know as
> much as possible about my audience today so I give useful infor-
> mation."). Company officials may be inviting new hires to your pre-
> sentation or reserving seats for middle management only. Ask!

2. Do you have directions to the conference or meeting place? (If
   not—get them.)

3. Do you know how long you're expected to speak? (If not, make a
   phone call and find out.)

4. Does your host organization know the title of your presentation?
   (Clarity on this matter is essential. If necessary, e-mail or fax the
   title of your speech along with a few sentences that should be used
   to introduce you to attendees.)

5. Are you dressed properly for this occasion? Will you need a jacket?
   (If you're not properly dressed, plan accordingly.)

6. Do you have handouts available on such short notice? If not, take
   a minute to consider whether something in your usual handouts
   will need to be explained to this audience. If so, take one handout with you. If you have a moment, use a highlighter to make
   priority information stand out.

> When John spoke, he referred to figures indicating the number of
> teenagers arrested for drunk driving in the last calendar year. He
> asked listeners to look at handouts for details surrounding those

numbers. He then asked for a few moments of silence while each person concentrated on the worrisome numbers. This portion of his presentation was powerful. When he didn't have handouts available to distribute to everyone, he made sure he had one handout to reference. He read some of the figures aloud. It was a second-best approach, but it was useful.

7. Are visual aids you typically use available and in excellent condition? (If not, do without them.)

8. Should you be eating lunch? Will it make you uncomfortable or edgy to miss a meal? (If so, eat something.)

9. Are you hydrated? (Take a bottle of water with you as you leave your office and drink it.)

10. Brush your teeth and enjoy a fresh breath mint. (Men may want to take a quick shave with the electric razor kept at the office for just such occasions.)

11. What will you say when you begin to speak?

Remember, you're not going to deliver the Gettysburg Address. But you'll want to have at least one clear point to introduce and discuss. Take care to crystallize that point in your thoughts before stepping up to the microphone.

12. What will you say when you end your presentation?

When time is too short to prepare a presentation as usual, prepare the beginning and the end. Keep it simple but say something of value when you close. If you want people to take action, change their opinions, learn something new, rally them to the task in your closing statement.

13. Will you conduct a Question and Answer session? (Don't introduce a Q&A segment unless you have the go-ahead from whoever is overseeing the entire program.)

14. Will you need to cancel other appointments when you accept this short-notice invitation? (Check your appointment calendar. Notify people of changes, if appropriate. Better still, ask a coworker to do this for you.) Not only is this the considerate thing to do, but it will save you from becoming distracted or upset by the gaffe if you suddenly remember the commitment as you're about to present.

15. When will you return to the office? Notify colleagues and interested parties when to expect your return. This small courtesy supports accurate communication among your coworkers, clients, customers, and vendors.

Last Minute Checklists

Before You Leave

Assemble the following items and put them in your briefcase—now. This is your Last Minute Checklist!

1. Notes with the name of your host organization, meeting address, contact person, and that person's cell phone number.

2. Directions to the destination. Time you're expected to arrive.

3. Printed introduction—to be used to introduce you to the audience.

4. One copy of a presentation handout you can refer to if needed. If you're speaking to a small group of people (6 to 12), ask someone to make copies of your handout when you arrive. Frequently, this is easy to do and doesn't cause anyone inconvenience.

5. Note cards with key words for your opening and closing remarks.

6. Publicity sheets—if you have them.

If you maintain a press kit, take one with you (make sure it's up-to-date). If you promote a company, product, service, or organization and have descriptive literature, take it with you. Any of these items should be handed to reporters, company newsletter editors, or other people who may report on your presentation. Ask these people if you can send anything to them when you return to your office. Just because you arrive to present on short notice doesn't mean you or your topic should be short-changed when it comes to media coverage.

7. Comb, brush, lipstick, breath fresheners, and if you need it—a deodorant.

8. A small tape recorder. Use it to record impressions or observations on your way home or back to the office.

When You Arrive

1. Slow down. (You've been in hurry-up mode to get to your destination. Put on the breaks!)

> Some last minute speakers are so intent upon returning to their chairs that they neglect to spend a moment or two in front of the audience basking in the applause that comes at the end of the presentation. Don't rush!

2. Take time to shake hands with people. Smile.

3. Take three or four deep breaths.

4. Say your opening remarks to yourself at least once before you speak to the group.

5. Step up to speak and remember—you have been called upon—people are friendly and happy you're here. Go get 'em!

Questions and Answers

1. You're the leader. Ask for questions that relate to the presentation and don't entertain questions about other topics. If you do, audience members are likely to lose interest.

2. Don't permit one attendee to "hold court" by asking numerous questions or making lengthy comments. Interrupt if necessary. Acknowledge people seated in different places in the room.

3. Listen to the entire question before you answer it.

4. When you're unsure of what the person wants, invite him or her to "tell me more." Wait to supply an answer until you're clear about the question.

5. Don't be too quick to say, "That's a great question." It suggests that the other questions asked aren't great.

6. Support your answers with facts and figures when possible.

7. When there's not a cast-in-stone answer to a question, preface your answers with the words, "In my opinion . . . "

8. Maintain eye contact with the questioner while he or she is speaking. You may opt to withhold eye contact if someone attempts to goad you.

9. If you walk around the audience handing a microphone to people who ask questions, make sure you retrieve it before you begin to answer.

It's important to hear everyone who speaks, but the person who has the microphone controls the conversation.

10. If the person asks a question without benefit of a microphone, repeat the question so everyone can hear it.

11. When you don't know an answer to a question, say so. You may want to offer to find the answer and contact the individual who asks it. If so, make sure you obtain contact information and then follow up.

12. Don't turn into a "lump" during the Q&A session. You may purposely be animated when you speak. Don't eliminate that persona now. An expressive face and hand motions will help boost the energy level in the room.

13. Keep breathing! Your voice can become high-pitched and sound "off" when you're so focused on providing answers that you start to take shallow breaths.

14. If you can introduce some levity to the answers you provide, by all means do so. Take care, however, not to make the questioner the butt of your humor.

15. Punctuate your answer with storytelling. Use good taste but don't be reluctant to get personal and specific.

Joan travels six months a year to clients' locations to help train their employees. She uses her on-the-road experiences to illustrate points.

Q: What happens when I arrange for a speaker to appear at an event my boss is hosting but the speaker is a no-show?

A: Be creative about assisting your speaker to reach you. Planes were stranded in Newark, New Jersey, during an August lightning storm. An artist friend of mine was stuck at the airport. He was scheduled to speak in Lenox, Massachusetts, at a breakfast meeting the following morning. The curator of the Norman Rockwell Museum was hosting a fund-raising event and wanted my friend to be there. He arranged for a relay of drivers to meet the artist and move him along. Someone picked up my friend at the airport and drove him to New York State. Another person met him and drove him to Connecticut. And a third "patron of the arts" met him and drove him to the destination. It took about six hours for the artist to reach Lenox, but he got there and gave his presentation.

Joan usually adds: "The impossible often takes a little longer to achieve!"

16. If an answer you provide is not understood—and people's body language will offer you a clue about this—ask the questioner if he or she has a follow-up question.

You may want to give attendees a way to contact you after the program concludes. Some speakers maintain e-mail addresses for this purpose. You may want to arrange for a link to your e-mail address to be added to the host company or organization's Web site. Invite attendees to use it.

17. When you "think" you know an answer and believe you can wing it, stop. Sometimes this approach is successful, but when it backfires, the fallout is disastrous.

18. Don't bring a Q&A to an abrupt end. "There's time for two more questions," is one way to conclude. Then stick to the plan—don't accept three questions.

19. Refrain from being verbose. When you're asked a question that's new to you, it's tempting to think aloud as you respond. If you do this, you're not likely to be brief and to the point. This is a surefire way to lose your audience's attention. You worked hard to keep everyone's attention. Don't blow it.

20. If you received some excellent questions, remember them. The next time you have to encourage people to ask questions, you may use one of them to stimulate participation.

Tips on Speaking Clearly

1. Don't rush and don't speak too slowly. How can you know what's considered too fast or too slow? Study the pace most people use in the geographic area in which you're making a presentation. Don't sacrifice clarity, but do try to mirror pace. Of course, if you're speaking on television or radio and will reach a wide audience, this tip won't apply.

People in metropolitan areas tend to speak more rapidly than those in low-population communities. Regional inflections affect understanding too. Some Bostonians ignore the *er* sound at the end of a word and substitute *ah*. They frequently ignore the r sound in words too. For example, butter sounds like *buttah*, and park sounds like *pahk*. You probably don't think you have an accent. Others may not agree. Should you get a voice coach to evaluate you?

2. Open your mouth! Speakers who feel tense often clench their jaws. Remember to open wide and let your words out.

3. Don't crowd the microphone. A microphone can amplify each breath you take and magnify small sounds the audience wouldn't otherwise hear.

4. Use the lavaliere microphone with care. These can be wired or wireless and you should dress appropriately to accommodate the lavaliere. You may want to wear something with a lapel or tie so the lavaliere mike can be clipped to it. If possible, ask about this in advance of your appearance so you'll be prepared.

If you're making a television appearance, rely upon the sound technician to place your microphone. Remember not to say anything inappropriate when the microphone is live (i.e., operative). Play it safe and don't say anything inappropriate—period.

5. No slouching, please. When your posture is poor, your words twist and turn to make their exit. This doesn't bode well for clarity.

6. Don't string words together unless you do so for a reason. "Fuhgetaboutit" is a corruption of three words. Utter them as one and expect to get a smile from listeners. Continue to string words together, however, and you will probably see puzzled looks on faces.

7. Some presentations are recorded. The recordings may be sold or distributed to attendees. Take advantage of these recorded sessions. Obtain the product and listen to yourself. Challenge yourself to find at least one thing you can do to sound better. Don't blame yourself for "perceived" errors if the recording quality is less than perfect.

8. When quoting an individual, be accurate. (Of course, you'll make the appropriate attribution.) Still, if you misrepresent someone because you transpose a number or omit an important word, you do that person and your listeners a disservice. When you don't speak clearly, the quote is as good as flubbed!

9. Visual aids "speak" too. Are they large enough to be seen by everyone in the room? Are they loaded with text or easy to read? Do they supplement what you're saying instead of repeating it? In short, this portion of your presentation "talks" to listeners. Make sure that what is "said" is well said.

10. Are you using the "active" voice? This permits you to communicate in a short, to-the-point style. It's far easier to communicate clearly when you're brief and to-the-point.

Passive vs. Active Voice

Passive = Action on the suggestion is being considered by the team.

Active = The team is considering action on the suggestion.

If you're not a grammarian and don't feel comfortable thinking about the active versus the passive voice, that's okay. Simply say it (whatever it is) short and to-the-point. Most of the time you'll be using the active voice.

11. When you're introducing technical terms to a nontechnical audience, help people out. If you mention sleep apnea to a group, you can then say, "Apnea? It means stop breathing." Even when you enunciate as perfectly as you can, listeners won't get a clear message when they're unfamiliar with a word's meaning.

12. When confidence is lacking, clarity is compromised. That's because the speaker isn't enthusiastic and tends to swallow words rather than project them. Listeners tune out. Why shouldn't they?

Key Presentation Skills

The following list was promised earlier, in the Introduction. Each topic has been discussed in some detail, and each is presented here in no particular order of importance. Some of the topics are obvious to most people, and others are shadowy. This list is not and should not be considered complete. It provides you with an at-a-glance opportunity to review significant do's and don'ts.

- **Know your audience.** This includes its objectives and capacity to understand your message.

- **Get their attention.** People are wooed by a multitude of messages and distractions. Hook them, fast!

- **Prepare to counter objections.** It's not practical to spend a long time preparing for objections that may never arise, but when you anticipate controversy, hone in on specifics and consider how to respond. Rehearse.

- **Select the main points.** Deliver the most important facts so they stand out. Too much information tends to water down important news.

- **Prove it.** Be ready with dependable evidence to support your facts. Cite sources.

- **Exhibit business etiquette.** Act in a proper fashion so your behavior supports you and contributes to your achieving your goals.

- **Control the audience.** A presenter is in a position of leadership. When questions and commentary are irrelevant, politely guide people to focus on the matter at hand.

- **Care about your audience.** If your true goal is to serve your audience, ask yourself what you can do for it. Then do it!

- **Don't undermine believability.** Exaggeration must be handled with care. Choose words cautiously, especially if you're making promises.

- **Build your confidence.** Banish self-doubt before you step up to the microphone. A positive attitude permits you to serve your audience better.

- **Use time wisely.** One major gaffe is showing visual aids to people who can't see them clearly. Presenters who waste an audience's time invite its ire.

- **Encourage people to believe.** "You gotta believe" is a phrase associated with the Phillies late, great, baseball star, Tug McGraw. In order to persuade people to be fearless, appeal to their faith.

- **Steal the thunder.** When you confess to a mistake or state the obvious, you usually move bad news into the open. You free listeners to acknowledge it and move on.

- **Know your topic.** By staying well-informed, you'll be able to counter objections, suggest remedies, and move in new directions as circumstances dictate.

- **Think the way the birds think.** Consider what the listener wants, and you'll be able to deliver the preferred bird seed!

- **Choose realistic objectives.** It may take more than a presentation to achieve your ultimate goal. You risk disappointment if you're unrealistic. Disappointment supports a chain of events that undermines success.

- **Use a microphone to amplify sound.** It can't add emotion, variation, or affect pace. Only you can do that.

- **Sharpen self-confidence.** Knowing you can stay on track with your speech because you've prepared clear and helpful notes is a confidence booster. Look for confidence boosters everywhere and use them.

- **Offer well-known facts to all assembled.** Find a common denominator to engage your audience and proceed from there.

- **Embrace the subtleties of body language.** Presenters who use body language subtleties (e.g., a handshake) add immeasurably to their ability to communicate effectively.

- **Appeal to the senses.** Sight, sound, touch, taste, and smell send messages too. For example, tasteful organ music helps to signal a solemn occasion.

- **Look for more than one way to get the job done.** Break with tradition if what you deliver is as good as or better than what has been done in the past.

- **Take care not to permit flattery to cloud your vision.** It's not unnatural to bask in the glow of receiving an invitation to speak. It's better to decline if, for any reason, you're unable to perform to your high standards.

- **Look good!** Dress for success! Take pains with hair care, choice of jewelry, use of fragrances, and all things that contribute to your appearance.

When 500 or More People Give You Their Attention

All the basics apply when you're speaking to larger crowds, but here are some additional things to consider in various situations:

- **Dais appearance.** Here's a scenario you may confront: You're a prominent speaker seated on a stage with several other well-known, capable speakers, and the arena is packed. Prepare to feel more tension than usual but *get over it*. Other than brief niceties (e.g., "Hello"), ignore the other speakers and focus on your delivery. Change nothing.

- **Television appearance.** Become familiar with the show and the host. If prudent, obtain taped copies of former shows and study them. Is the host's style provocative? Is he or she a stickler for details? Does the host cut off speakers or permit them to finish?

  Lyn was about to sign books and conduct a Sunday seminar at a major bookstore. A public relations expert arranged for her appearance on two morning talk shows. She knew the venue was friendly and that she would answer questions about her latest book. The week before her television appearances, she purchased a new jacket and jewelry. To see how she "felt" in the outfit, she wore it to a business luncheon, where she received compliments: "You look terrific!" She believed this also had something to do with the whitening strips she'd been using on her teeth. Lyn's television appearance preparation centered on her "looks." Since television cameras are extremely revealing and since everything else was "comfortable," it was the sensible thing to do.

- **Radio.** Frequently, the person making a radio presentation isn't in a studio. He or she may be seated at home speaking to a radio personality, and the listening audience, via telephone. Dress-up is optional! Some presenters prefer to be dressed for the occasion. They believe this helps them exude self-confidence.

Also, you can read from your notes, but take care not to sound as though you're reading. It's agreeable to take notes when the host asks questions. Refer to them when you answer questions.

You can sip water, but don't chew food or suck candy. (Close the door to your room and make sure Fido is out of range.)

All the usual presentation rules apply with the exception of those that apply when you're visible!

- **Reporters' interview.** You may be answering reporters' questions in a casual setting, but whatever you say is subject to being reported to thousands of readers. In addition, the reporter(s) will pick and choose what to report and what to omit, and you may conclude there's nothing casual about this presentation opportunity.

  Reporters don't typically conduct an interview using a list of preconceived questions. You can exercise a certain amount of control when you use word combinations that stand out because they provoke follow-up questions. You'll probably want to give illustrations (i.e., tell stories) to prove points. Take care not to offend any group or to ramble. If you want to check facts, ask the reporter: "Can I get back to you?" It's rare that this works, so take care to use words such as: *estimated, about, at last count was,* etc. Reporters frequently go to more than one source, and if you say something that is widely refuted by other sources, you'll probably regret it.

Chapter Three

How Did I Do?

No matter how many times you have given a presentation, there's always room for improvement. This chapter provides what you need to make sure your next presentation is even better than your last.

Was your voice pleasant? Did you make meaningful eye contact? Was your material logical and easy to follow? Did you make attendees smile? Could you feel the energy level in the room lift as you progressed from point to point? And about questions: Were they asked? Did you answer them to everyone's satisfaction? Did you end on time?

Specific answers to these questions and dozens more will assist you to answer the big question: "How did I do?"

Ever hear the one about the man who asked, "How do I get to Carnegie Hall?" and the New York City pedestrian who replied, "Practice, practice, practice"? If you plan to be among the best speakers, this advice will help you arrive at your destination. But what should you practice?

Feedback, Please

Danny, a medical instruments sales representative, was told by his boss that he should consider wearing business suits when he made presentations. He started to purchase his business wardrobe at a fashionable men's clothing store. After time passed, he noticed that audiences took him more seriously, and something else happened too. Everyone took him more seriously whether he was making a presentation or just going to lunch with colleagues.

Mary, a temporary employment agency owner, knew she was too soft spoken and that it worked against her when she trained new employees.

Her goal was to speak in a more robust fashion. It didn't happen until one day when her partner said, "Mary, why not take singing lessons?"

As these illustrations suggest, unsolicited feedback can be both welcome and helpful. Ask yourself, however, if you readily provide speakers with constructive criticism. You may be reluctant to do so for fear of offending someone. Or you may believe they don't want to hear it. No doubt others feel this way too.

According to Michel de Montaigne (1513–1592), a French philosopher and writer, "We need very strong ears to hear ourselves judged frankly, and because there are few who can endure frank criticism without being stung by it, those who venture to criticize us perform a remarkable act of friendship. . . ."

Looking for Friendship

You don't have to sit around and wait for friends to show up. Go ahead and solicit feedback. Ask the "right" questions and use tactful phrases, and most of what you receive will be constructive criticism.

Use Surveys

Distribute short survey forms at the end of your program. Encourage people to fill them in and return them. When they're anonymous (i.e., you don't ask for a name or a signature), people are more likely to cooperate and be candid.

The topic of surveys, how to prepare them, what to expect from them, and everything about them is the stuff of which entire books are written. You can make a lifetime study of the topic or you can KISS (Keep It Short/Simple). Choose from some of the specific questions that appear in this chapter and see if the responses you receive are useful. If, for example, you speak to 20 people and 10 of them cooperate by filling in and returning your survey and half of them say something similar—that could be something you'll want to assign a priority status to. "Couldn't hear you from the back of the room," or, "I didn't receive a handout. There weren't enough to go around." If these answers or variations on them came about as a result of questions (Could you hear the presentation? Are the handouts of value?), it doesn't take a rocket scientist to recognize you've got useful feedback. Use it!

Interview One or More Attendees

It's not unusual for some people to stay and chat with the speaker when others exit. Even though you're now in your relaxed mode, use the time constructively. These people are able to tell you "a story" that isn't likely to be captured via a survey.

Dropouts Count Too

If you're engaged in presenting ongoing programs (e.g., training workshops, Webinars), it's highly unlikely that everyone remains in the program from beginning to end. If possible, solicit feedback from dropouts. Of course, if someone leaves in the middle of a presentation that's not part of an ongoing "package," his or her feedback is valuable too. But it may not be practical to obtain this individual's cooperation to evaluate the program. Someone who made a longer-term commitment, however, may be pleased to supply feedback.

Presenters may consider it a personal affront when people walk out on a presentation. Sometimes people leave because of extenuating circumstances, but other times they leave because they just don't like the program. Did you do something that sent them packing? Ask! You miss a golden opportunity if you neglect to assess failures.

Ask, "What could I have done that would have kept you with us until the end?" And: "On a scale from 1 to 10, can you tell me how you rate the program? I know you won't rate it as high as 10 because you didn't stay until the end." Most people don't feel comfortable with dead air (i.e., silence). If you say only a little to this person and wait, he or she is likely to give you an evaluation of some kind, such as:

"It wasn't what I expected. You gave information that's too basic (or too advanced)."

"The room was stuffy, and I got a headache."

"Your voice is putting me to sleep. It's probably my fault, but I decided to leave. I have important things waiting for me at the office." (You've just been told the program is unimportant.)

Arrange for Feedback at the Outset

Pepper the audience with some listeners who are actively seeking bumps in your presentation. Your partner, for example, may give you a useful assessment of the opening and end of your program. A coworker may focus on organization: Was the presentation well organized?

Be specific. If you simply ask, "Was it a good program?" you may not learn much that you can use. On the other hand, if you ask one person to simply focus on your body language and you learn that you frequently put your hands up to push your hair out of your eyes, you'll probably adopt a different hairstyle next time you speak. Obtain specific information and be ready to make specific changes. Of course if you hear, "Your opening statement got everyone's attention. A hush fell over the room as soon as you got the first words out of your mouth," you'll take specific steps to hang onto those words and that opening for future use. Nothing but the facts, please!

Test Your Props

These inanimate objects will supply feedback if you know how to obtain it. Are you using a slide program? If so and if you can view slides in black and white, look at them to obtain feedback. Good design should look good in black and white. If black and white slides don't have any oomph, it's likely they won't have much more oomph when shown in color. It's too easy to fall in love with program enhancements you select and have become comfortable with—try to fall out of love. If you can be wooed away, it's likely the slide program, flip chart, handouts, musical background, or whatever, can be made better.

Even though you make judgments about your presentation all the time, finding new ways to evaluate the "commonplace" can assist you in fine-tuning your presentation. The scrutiny of slides in black and white is one way to do this.

Another way is to sit in the back of the room and look at visual aids. Can you see them? Would bolder colors hold your attention better? Do you distribute name tags? If so, can they be read with ease? If not, why are you supplying them? Be on the lookout for making all things better.

Coaches and Mentors

Use coaches and mentors to evaluate your performance, but that doesn't mean you just sit there and take it. You can initiate the evaluation. "How can I sound more authoritative?" Fred asked his voice coach. She had trained him to speak in a lower register, but he felt there was more he could do. Much to his surprise, she said, "It's not your spoken language—it's your body language." She didn't know being authoritative was a concern of his until he asked.

Q&A Time Can Provide Clues

The questions you receive can expose weaknesses and strengths in your program. Max, a computer programmer and trainer, found that when there were the same frequently asked questions, something was amiss. Programmers in several different states asked about the unusual color coding on a newly introduced keyboard his company developed. Why were they all asking? Should he cover the topic better when he spoke?

He didn't try to answer this question on his own. He sought input from his boss and a manager in the design department. Now the process had come full circle. He sifted the questions he received and asked his colleagues to help him assess the situation. In this instance, it was decided to provide Max with handouts that touted the benefits of the new and different color coding system.

Know Your Tools

If you use a projector, is it the most suitable projector for your needs? It might have been when you obtained it a few years ago, but there may be projectors that would serve you better today. Do you travel to speaking engagements with a microphone you own? Does it serve you well? Seek feedback from people who sell projectors, microphones, or other tools of your trade. Leading edge technology often makes excellent tools available to us, and the cost of these is often not prohibitive. You may never discover this in a timely fashion unless you go shopping.

No need to jump on a train and head for the city when it's time to go shopping for presentation tools. You have more options today than ever before when you want to check on the tools of your trade. Magazines, the Internet, and specialized e-newsletters provide new product announcements, specifications, and prices, and they may even offer trial periods so you can try before you buy. Of course, you may want to jump on that train, get into your car, or visit shops that cater to speakers. But remember that although salespeople are good feedback providers, they'll feature the benefits, so you'll have to probe with questions that help you ferret out the rest of the story.

Confer with Speaker Peers

Sometimes the competition is willing to share information because it'll get as good as it'll give. If you make your living as a motivational speaker, for example, you may want to contact other motivational speakers and chat. Some will consider you the "enemy"—surely you represent the competition. But others realize there's sufficient work for everyone and you can support one another as each of you perfects presentation skills:

"How did audiences on college campuses in Georgia and Alabama respond to you?

"Did you have to change your approach when you spoke to CEOs of Fortune 500 companies recently? I'm thinking those folks may be more sophisticated and I might need to redo my presentation when I speak to a similar group next month."

Few competitors, if any, do precisely what you do. The occasional information exchange could benefit each of you. And if you find it "lonely out there," it could be that other presenters agree and would be happy to know they can "bounce off you" when necessary. A mutually beneficial dialogue can have long-lasting positive effects.

Sample Questions to Elicit Feedback

All About Content

1. Did you learn something today you didn't know before?

2. How will you use the information you obtained?

3. Was the presentation too long, too short, or just right? How did you come to your conclusion?

4. Did anything I say confuse you?

5. On a scale of 1 to 10 for "easy to understand content," would you rate the presentation a high of 10? Please explain your choice.

All about Environment

1. Was the room temperature comfortable?

2. Could you hear the presentation with ease?

3. Do you prefer the table seating arrangement used today? What do you like or dislike about it?

4. Would you like more or less break time? Why?

5. If applicable: Did you find it easy to travel to this location?

All about Visual Aids

1. Were the slides (or specific visual aids) useful? In what way?

2. Did you have sufficient time to read or study them? If not, should I show fewer slides?

3. Should each slide contain more or less information?

4. Was the commentary that accompanied slides distracting, and, if so, what suggestions can you make to improve the visual portion of the presentation?

5. Would the presentation have been as good or better without visual aids? Please explain why.

All about Me

1. Did I speak clearly, or did you miss hearing some of what I said?

2. Did I make you feel comfortable about asking questions or making comments?

3. I realize that an attendee spends a lot of time looking at the speaker, so I hope you don't mind if I ask: Do I look okay? Is there anything about my personal appearance I should change for the benefit of listeners?

4. Do you think I know my topic well? If not, what did I say, or not say, that makes you think so?

5. If you were trying to decide to attend another workshop and learned that I was the presenter, would that influence your decision? Please explain.

All about This and That

1. Do you think the admission fee is reasonable?

2. On a personal level: Did you have fun, and if not, why not?

3. You received the speaker's e-mail address. Will you use it?

4. Do you think the many illustrations the speaker used will help you remember information and how to use it?

5. What was the best thing about this presentation? What was the worst thing?

Don't forget to thank participants for giving you feedback.

> Act like a sponge and absorb information you obtain. Make note of answers and keep them available for future reference. If you don't, gathering the information is a waste of time.

Chapter Four

Moving On to Your Next Presentation

Since you'll probably be asked to give many presentations throughout your career, this chapter spotlights smart presentation strategies for reusing or "recycling" material you used before, in order to save you time and effort. Learn how to use the same wording and visuals for your next speech—even if it's on a different topic. These tips and strategies rescue you from unnecessary work and time spent reinventing the wheel.

> The powers-that-be at a junior high school warn students not to use the same speech for "more than one school year." These officials claim that the intent of the rule is to prevent a student from using research and content more than once, making only minor changes. In effect, this faculty testifies to the wisdom of our plan to get full value from research and writing by making only minor changes— and using the same speech over and over again.

In Chapter One of Part 2 we discuss the seven Quick Keys to a successful presentation. Each of those keys is discussed below, with additional points as well, including tips and strategies for recycling former presentations.

It's about Time

Organize

Pause for a moment to consider the etymology of the word *organize*. It's from the Latin *organum*, which means "tool" or "instrument" (*The American Heritage Dictionary of the English Language*, Fourth Edition, 2000). When copies of your speeches are in folders and the folders are clearly labeled and accessible, pertinent resource material will be available to you without delay. The value of this "tool" is incalculable.

Organization is not an easy thing for everyone. If you feel challenged in this arena, get help. It's possible that other aspects of your "world" need organizing too. What about your desk, office space, closets? Some people make a living by helping others to organize. You may not need to hire a professional organizer if a friend or colleague is able to assist you.

Categorize Creatively

When you set up files and folders or keep track of the location of materials via computer, be especially attentive to the headings you assign. For example, if you speak to audiences about planning for retirement, you may want to separate information on investment opportunities. Certificates of Deposit, Savings Accounts, and Real Estate Investments are three possible headings for folders.

Having categorized your affairs in this manner, if at some future time you're asked to make a presentation about how to save for a dream vacation, you'll be able to reach for related files and glean useful information for this audience. You will have the facts that back up the statement: "Don't invest in long-term Certificates of Deposit when you're earmarking those funds to pay for your vacation. You'll need to make a deposit on your cruise or tour months in advance of the actual travel date." Or you'll have the facts to back up this statement: "If your savings account balance dips too low, you may forfeit high interest earnings. If you use some of these savings to pay for your dream vacation, be aware of the impact withdrawals have on earnings."

Read and Rip

Scan these folders periodically and get rid of information that's dated or not used. If the contents of a number of files are obsolete, why waste time handling them?

Devote Limited Space to Maintaining Files

Ever notice how "stuff" grows to fill the space you devote to it? Be miserly with the space you assign to the task, and you'll find you store less. As a result it's easier to review saved information quickly.

It's about the Audience

Assess Your Audience after an Event

Tape record your assessment of the audience on your way home from an event and label the tape so it's quickly recognizable: Sales Staff, Community Leaders, Political Gatherings, etc. The next time you make a presentation to any of these audience types, listen to that recording. You'll be reminded if they were quick to grasp information, needed handholding, weren't interested, and so on. Establish a retention calendar. Is five years the length of time you can rely upon audience response to be similar? If so, destroy tapes that are older than five years of age.

Include the Name of Your "Go-to" Person

When you label the tapes you record after an event, include the name of your audience contact. For example, if Danny Smith was your host for the occasion, jot down, "Danny Smith, Director," on the tape. If you're invited to speak to this group or a "twin" group in the not too distant future, contact Danny. You might ask him, for instance: "Should I be aware of any changes that have taken place in your industry or anything in particular that would influence attendees' way of thinking?" If Danny is inclined to talk, listen to his assessment. A five- to ten-minute telephone conversation can provide you with a wealth of information about your current audience.

It's about Your Topic

If your listeners are going to feel any of the passion you feel for your topic, you have to show them how they benefit. In short, you must think the way the birds think. (This dictum, born a long time ago in the world of advertising, continues to be on target.)

Dave frequently spoke to social workers on the topic of autism. He emphasized services available to parents of children diagnosed with autism. The information he offered to this audience was well received because many social workers interact with young parents facing this challenge.

As the CEO of a Fortune 500 company, Dave took every opportunity to speak to executives whose companies could donate money to support autism research. How would executives benefit from supporting autism research? Surely, they could choose from dozens of other good causes to support.

Dave maintained a file folder labeled "Benefits List" and kept separate pages in the file entitled "Parents, Service Providers, and Donors." He scheduled 10 minutes of time on Monday mornings to review and add to those lists when he found something new to add. The donors would be more interested in the staggering number of children diagnosed and how this affected the medical costs. The parents would be more interested in knowing how to treat their children. Service providers needed to know about special needs physicians and organizations that served this population. Each of these groups would have some interest in the big picture, but Dave needed to "think the way the birds think." Parents, for example, would quickly lose interest in his presentation if he were to forecast a dismal future for their children and the demands they would make on the medical costs of the community.

> Devote three to four minutes to the following exercise now: Name two different groups that would be candidates for a favorite presentation you offer. Name one benefit for each group. Cross-check to determine if the other group would care. It's better if the answer is no. In a short amount of time you should find ways to please different groups. Don't accept speaking engagements for an audience that won't benefit from your presentation.

It's about You Too

If you "fit" one audience, you "fit" them all. Your speaking voice, pitch, pace, choice of vocabulary, ability with a microphone, as well as your personal appearance, grooming skills, body language, visual aids selections, good manners—when all the components meet high standards, they are welcomed by any audience. They are the basics. But why should anyone listen to you? What makes you an authority?

When Dave, in our last example, spoke to audiences, he never failed to mention that two of his grandchildren were diagnosed as moderately autistic. The children were diagnosed before the age of two, and they were now six and seven years old. Once people know this, they have every reason to believe Dave is passionate and well-informed, and is someone who believes in positive outcomes. They want to listen to him, and they assume that the information he provides is accurate.

It's about the Words

Can you recycle words? Yes, the fact is, you do it every day, but now, in a presentation, you can make a conscious effort to track words that meet the needs of one audience better than those of another audience. And while you're at it, take note of words that appeal to all audiences. Keep a Word

List in one of those folders you maintain. Glance at it from time to time and add to it when a particular word or group of words, or adjectives or adverbs, "sound" good to you. Here are some examples:

- Maxine made sure the word *you* was included in every opening statement she made when giving a speech. It was an easy rule to follow because she delivered conversational speeches. It's difficult to carry on a conversation without saying *you*.

- George keeps lists of action words (*jump, flight, pitch, catch*). He speaks to athletes, coaches, and sporting goods manufacturers, and these words help make his presentations energetic and positive, especially when he teams them with lively adjectives (spectacular jump, amazing flight, powerful pitch, controlled catch). He scans Word Lists prior to an engagement and asks himself, "Did I overlook anything?" For the most part, they can all be used for any audience. He keeps his Word Lists short. If he didn't, he would feel overwhelmed and not bother to consult them. In addition, it guarantees that anything that makes the list is worthy of consideration. He is cautious when using pronouns.

- Debbie sold a new house to Sue in November. She moved in December. (Did Debbie move or did Sue move?)

- Ramon transferred deeds to his son before leaving for Mexico. He neglected to notify Susan, and Ramon's son was upset when he found out. (Was Ramon's son upset after he found out that Susan wasn't notified or was Ramon upset?) When you're not clear and your listener is confused, it's easy for the listener to lose interest, daydream, or exit the room.

- Connie does crossword puzzles. When she finds what she considers an interesting word, she adds it to her Word List. A successful speaker, Connie has a habit of using alliteration and other powerful word "tricks." She challenges herself to use one new interesting word within the first few lines of any speech. It's a strategy that helps her feel energetic: "It keeps things fresh and new even when I've said it all before." The word *frisson*, explained as "a moment of intense excitement, a shudder, an emotional thrill," qualifies as "interesting." Another? *Antidisestablishmentarianism.* (Check your dictionary for the meaning.) The Web site www.Dictionary.com offers to e-mail a Word of the Day, without charge, to anyone who makes this request. Of course, all words won't necessarily qualify as interesting. It's up to you to determine which words you want to save and use.

- Keep track of stories you have told and the response you received. Recycle stories that elicited the most response or interest. If you can't track them in your memory, go ahead and create another list, titling it, for instance, "Picture Painting Stories." Of course, not all successful stories will be well received by all audiences. Karen sold property insurance and when she addressed groups of senior citizens, she didn't discuss motorcycles. She saved her motorcycle stories for groups of young men who were 20 to 40 years old. Insurance statistics indicate that these people own more motorcycles than do other groups.

A Few Words on Being Politically Correct

Take care not to offend anyone or any group. When speaking of African Americans, for example, can you use the term "black"? When speaking of homosexuals, can you use the term "gay"? What about "lesbian"? It's prudent to make note of sensitivities when you encounter them.

For example, Roscoe was engaged by a prestigious graduate school to recruit students, and he spoke to fraternity and sorority members about preparing themselves for international banking and investment jobs. He soon learned that on some campuses the reference to "frats" was not appreciated. He was told to say "Greek organizations" or "Greeks." He also discovered that references to "American Indian" and "Native American" were usually considered synonymous, but a specific reference to Navajo, Hopi, or Cherokee was "safer" still.

Roscoe traveled throughout the country and abroad to make presentations, and he found it useful to keep a few notes on words and phrases that were politically correct, as well as on terms that were considered offensive. He was surprised to discover, for instance, that gender sensitivities prevailed in some geographic areas of the United States. Instead of saying "mailman," he was advised to say "postal carrier." Instead of saying "waiter" or "waitress," he was advised to say "server." He felt some of these preferences were trendy and wouldn't last or become widely accepted. But he adapted the adage, "When in Rome, do as the Romans do." The few notes he maintained on the subject served as a memory jog when he once again appeared in a particular location.

It's about a Logical Flow

You don't need a dedicated folder to track logic—simply use a highlighter to mark copies of the speeches you've already delivered. Highlight main points. You may want to use different colors to show one point (yellow), then the next (blue).

When you're recycling a speech, you'll want to be sure to omit nothing that would impede logical flow. And you'll want to be sure not to add extraneous material. The color scan makes it quick and easy to compare the new against the old. If yellow and blue rotate throughout the speech, an orderly flow is in place. If yellow follows yellow and blue shows up here and there, it's likely that something is out of order. Your new audience may need a tidbit of information you neglected to mention, which doesn't bode well for you or them. Take an extra few moments to reexamine your recycled speech and fill in omissions if necessary.

It's about Less Is Best

You may want to use the color red, signifying *stop*, and attach a dab of it to each folder you maintain. It serves as a reminder to speak "short." Embellishment can be boring. It's possible that in the time since you gave the first presentation and now—when you're about to recycle it—you've learned more and have new stories to illustrate points, so it's easy to get hoodwinked into blah blah blah. *Stop.*

Personalize Recycle Folders as Needed

If there's something you know you need to be reminded of—retain it. One possible folder to add to the rest is: Wardrobe. Photographs tell the story quickly. If a photograph is taken on the occasion of your appearance, write the time and place on it and retain it in the applicable folder.

For example, Judith was a nurse who sometimes appeared in front of audiences dressed in her uniform. But occasionally she wore a business suit. She could appear wearing her uniform over and over but was sensitive about not wearing the same business suit in front of the same audience more than once. Nor did she want to appear in the same outfit when speaking in the same town in front of a different audience.

Judith maintained a diary that noted jewelry, shoes, and accessories she wore to a presentation,. She consulted it before dressing for a new presentation. In addition to avoiding the same "look" in the same venue, these reminders helped her buy new wardrobe and accessory items that complemented her appearance. Five years into her speaking appearances, she purchased business suits in brown and blue. Gone were the green and black clothing of earlier days. She attributed these preferences to being cognizant of what she wore on occasions when she got the most applause, i.e., the most positive feedback.

Create and use any folders you find helpful, but don't overload your files with too much information. Keep them lean, and they will remain inviting to use. In no time at all you'll have pertinent information—all in one place—enabling you to quickly get up to speed for your next presentation.

Recycle Visual Aids

In order to recycle visual aids, it's essential to keep them in pristine condition. If a slide is slightly bent, reject it. If a PowerPoint program has dated information, update it or delete it. If you've obtained new and pertinent information since the last time you made a presentation of this type, use it. In other words, feel free to recycle photographs, slides, graphs, charts, and handouts if doing so is timely and the material is in top condition.

One way to keep materials in top condition is to store them with care. And, as with written material, you'll want to catalog information efficiently so you can identify items and retrieve them quickly. Adopt an approach that meets your needs. An audiovisual team, within or outside of your company, should be able to make valuable recommendations. A knowledgeable clerk at an office supply store or photography shop can probably direct you to storage containers, albums, and the like. You'll want to make sure that temperatures in storage rooms are not too hot or too cold. And, most important, don't wait until the last minute to assemble and examine visual aids you plan to use. Review all of these items in private before you introduce them to an audience.

20 Smart Things to Do When Recycling a Speech

Note: The items in this list are in no particular order of importance.

- Arrive prepared. If necessary arrive early to check on the room and your equipment (e.g., microphone, projector).

- Dress appropriately, and if in doubt, dress up rather than dress down (i.e., formal versus casual or relaxed).

- Do nothing that would require you to apologize. ("Sorry, these handouts include information from a different presentation.")

- Know your material. Don't plan to read a recycled speech to your audience. The only time reading is permissible is when you're reading a short quote.

- Rely upon note cards to jog your memory, if you must. Glance at them as unobtrusively as possible. The way you prepare the cards will greatly determine their value to you. Jot key words only. Don't write too many words on one card. Write legibly and large enough so you can pick up information without squinting at the cards.

- Speak correctly. Not only should sentences be grammatically correct, but they should be clear. Say what you mean and mean what you say!

- Carry copies of your introduction with you. Check with the person who will introduce you to the audience to see if he or she wants a copy. If important information isn't mentioned (e.g., you have an advanced degree or special certification in the topic you're discussing), tell the audience yourself. The earlier you do, the better. You can then forget about it, and the audience is privy to that information as it listens to you speak.

- Remember, you're familiar with everything you are about to say, but the audience isn't! Even if you have recycled this presentation many times over, you must keep it fresh. This is especially true if you're a trainer. Even though you feel passionate about the material, stay alert to avoid making a singsong delivery or hurrying through some parts of the presentation.

- Make sure you get a good night's sleep, eat properly, and exercise, if that's your habit. It's helpful to be physically fit as well as mentally prepared for this occasion.

- Be ready to interpret visuals for your audience. Don't assume audience members can immediately grasp the meaning of graphs and charts. This may be a good time to interact with listeners—ask people if they understand: "Does anyone question why the March figures are lower than the April figures?" You should be able to quickly ascertain if more explanation is required. And if some of your visual aids repeatedly need detailed explanations, it may be time to redesign rather than recycle them.

- Stand where you can be seen easily by everyone in the audience, and be careful not to block visual aids or items you want your audience to see.

- Practice using laser pointers or similar tools just prior to using them. Sometimes batteries or bulbs need replacing. The time to do this is before your presentation begins.

- If it's practical, meet and greet attendees as they enter the room. Introduce yourself and exchange small talk. "This is a lovely facility. I've never been here before. Have you?" Later you may feel more comfortable making eye contact with friendly faces. Take care not to let one individual monopolize your attention. Don't get so involved in conversation that you neglect to start the program on time.

- Don't speak for longer than planned. If you're completely in charge of the program, make sure to announce break time so people can use restrooms, make phone calls, etc. Be clear about the time you will start speaking again. If some people are slow to return to the room, use your judgment about waiting for them. Generally, you'll want to stick to the announced time so you can finish the session on time and not omit material.

- Familiarize yourself with handouts. If you recycle handouts without reading them, you may not remember details. This can be embarrassing if someone asks questions about something mentioned in the handout.

- Artificially heated or cooled meeting rooms tend to have dry air that can make a speaker hem, haw, and cough. See to it that you have a glass of water available before you begin to speak. Step away from the microphone before you take a sip of water.

- If you're presenting a longer program, you may be tempted to remove your tie or jacket as the day moves on. Think carefully about whether you should. Make your decision based upon how this might affect your image.

- Be mindful of room temperatures, the availability of water, pads, pencils, and anything else that affects the comfort of attendees. It's likely that someone else will be in charge of these matters, but you're affected by how well your audience fares. One of the benefits of returning to a location to give a presentation is that a track record has been established. If the environment left something to be desired in the past, you may want to inquire about conditions before the speaking date. Speak to someone who has the authority to make a difference. Ask for assurances that everything will be handled in a satisfactory manner this time.

- Ask for feedback. Will you want to change the survey you used in the past? Take advantage of the opportunity to build on what you learned last time. You might have asked, for instance, "With whom will you use the information you obtained today?" And perhaps you offered multiple choices such as coworkers, clients, and people in business as well as in personal life. On this occasion, you might repeat the same question but change the multiple-choice options. Take the time to consider how you will benefit from information you obtain from a survey—then ask your audience for that feedback.

- Did you literally run out of steam at the end of the presentation last time? If so, be ready to go out with a roar now. Or if you were pleased with your finale last time, be ready to repeat it. In short, put thought and energy into the good-bye part of your presentation. You'll want to leave attendees with something to think about or act upon. You want the experience to change them in some way. And you may just want to be invited back!

Don't recycle a presentation for an audience that heard you speak a short time ago. Write new material. Refer to key points, but offer new illustrations to make them stick!

Index

Index

About the Author

Marilyn Pincus has written books and articles for the major publishers of business information, including McGraw-Hill, Barron's Educational Series, Inc., Prentice-Hall, Simon & Schuster, Kaplan Publishing, and Adams Media. Her books have been translated into the Portuguese, Danish, Spanish, and Korean languages, and two versions of the Chinese language.

Based near Phoenix, Arizona, she operates Marilyn Pincus, Inc. She's a member of the prestigious Authors Guild headquartered in New York City, the International Association of Business Communicators in San Francisco, and theWomen's Studies Advisory Council (WOSAC) at the University of Arizona.